√ **W9-ANB-146**

THE BERLIN WALL

THE BERLIN WALL

HOW IT ROSE AND WHY IT FELL

DORIS M. EPLER

The Millbrook Press
Brookfield, Connecticut

Maps by Joe LeMonnier

Photographs courtesy of: German Information Center: pp. 13, 44 (both), 73 (both), 79, 88; Bettmann Archive: pp. 17, 20, 25, 33, 39, 48, 63, 67, 97, 99 (both), 108; AP/ Wide World: pp. 54, 55, 58, 94, 115.

Library of Congress Cataloging-in-Publication Data

Epler, Doris M.
The Berlin Wall : how it rose and why it fell / by Doris M. Epler.
p. cm.
Includes bibliographical references and index.
Summary: A history of the much hated wall that for nearly thirty years divided Berlin and created two separate countries.
ISBN 1-56294-114-3
1. Berlin Wall, Berlin, Germany, 1961–1989—Juvenile literature.
2. Berlin (Germany)—History—1945–1990—Juvenile literature.
3. Germany—History—1945–1990—Juvenile literature. [1. Berlin Wall, Berlin, Germany, 1961–1989.] I. Title.
DD881.E65 1992
943.1'55—dc20   91-20610 CIP AC

This book was made possible with the help of the following
persons who shared resources, provided advice and counsel,
and gave me encouragement to complete the work:

Mary Ann Achorn, Hershey Middle School Library;

Celeste DiCarlo Nalwasky, Peters Township Middle School Library;

Phillip Hearne, Hershey Public Library;

Charles Puguese, Harrisburg Area Community College;

the staff of the State Library of Pennsylvania;

Mary Ann Brenner, Swatara Junior/Senior High School Library;

Debra Kachel, Ephrata High School Library;

Mara Anderson, Ephrata Area School District;

the staff of Dauphin County Library;

Jean Tuzinski, Pennsylvania Department of Education;

A. J. Toth, a special friend; and

Geraldine Wagner, a sister who willingly served as my motivator.

Doris M. Epler

CONTENTS

To my grandchildren

Joseph, Donna, Sherry,
Jonathan, and Jeffrey
May a wall never divide
the peoples of your world!

Nanna

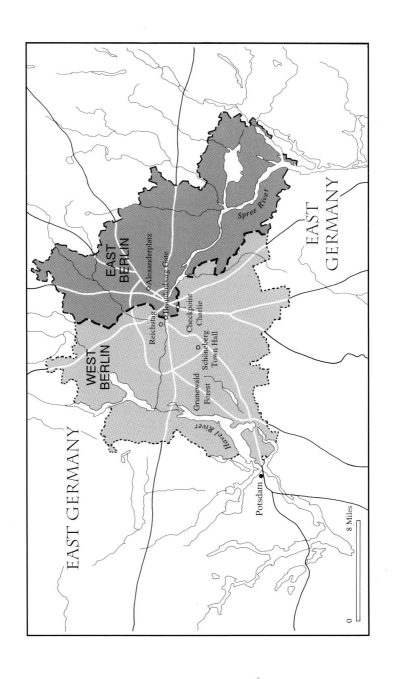

EAST GERMANY

EAST GERMANY

EAST BERLIN

WEST BERLIN

Spree River

Havel River

Alexanderplatz
Brandenburg Gate
Reichstag
Checkpoint Charlie
Schöneberg Town Hall
Grunewald Forest

Potsdam

0   8 Miles

CHAPTER ONE
BEFORE THE WALL

Imagine, if you can, waking up some morning to find a wall running down the center of the main street of your town, cutting your city in half. No one may cross from one side to the other, regardless of family situations, jobs, or schooling. To do so would be to risk death. Furthermore, imagine that on one side of the wall people are permitted to do all the normal things that free people expect to do, and they may go and come at will. But on the other side many freedoms are taken away from the people.

This is what happened in the city of Berlin, once the proud capital of Germany, in 1961. The Berlin Wall was erected by the Communist government of East Germany to keep East German citizens from escaping to the West. It stood for twenty-eight years—a symbol of repression that became known as the Wall of Shame. Hundreds of people died trying to cross it. Thousands of lives were disrupted.

The story of how Berlin became a divided city—and how it was made whole again—begins long before the Wall was built. The rise and fall of the Berlin Wall cannot be understood without a look back into the history of Germany.

Germany Between the Wars ▪ In 1918, Germany was defeated by the Allies, including the United States, Britain, and France, in World War I. The country had lost about two million soldiers, and millions more had been wounded. Its ruler, Kaiser Wilhelm II, was driven into exile by a popular uprising. Germany itself, however, had escaped serious war damage.

Berlin at this time was a large and enormously beautiful city, covering more than 340 square miles. It was a wonderfully green city, with glorious trees, forest-rimmed lakes, and the Spree River running through its center. The city included outlying farm areas, and much of its land was covered with pine and birch forests. In the city center were broad, tree-lined boulevards and narrow streets and alleys, lined with stone apartment buildings and many small businesses. With more outdoor monuments and statues than Rome, and more bridges than Venice, it ranked as one of the finest cities in the world. Among its more famous buildings was the Reichstag, an enormous stone edifice where the German parliament first met in 1871. The Brandenburg Gate, an impressive monument with huge Doric columns flanked by twin temple pavilions, stood near the city center on one of Berlin's most famous boulevards, Unter den Linden (Under the Lindens).

But along with the rest of Germany, Berlin faced hard times after World War I. Although U.S. President Woodrow Wilson promised a reasonable peace settle-

*In the years before World War II, Berlin was known
as one of Europe's most beautiful capital cities.*

ment, France and Britain wanted Germany punished. In the end, under the Treaty of Versailles, Germany was forced to give up much territory and pay the Allies $33 billion in reparations, or payments for war damage. Many Germans were bitter.

A new German government, known as the Weimar Republic, was formed in 1919. This government proved to be weak and incompetent, and Germany was unable to make its reparations payments. As a result, in 1923, French troops seized the rich coal mines in Germany's Ruhr Valley, to try to force the Germans to meet their obligation. The German government encouraged the coal miners to strike, so that the French would not be able to operate the mines. To support the striking miners financially, Germany printed additional currency for which it had no backing. And this fueled inflation (rising prices), which had already been increasing.

Soon factories were churning out almost worthless currency that had shrunk in value a billion times. In U.S. currency, that would mean a shopper would need $1 billion to buy something that had previously cost one dollar. German workers had to take their pay home in wheelbarrows. Savings became worthless overnight.

By 1924, new leaders had succeeded in stabilizing the currency. Germans enjoyed a brief time of relative prosperity. But in 1929 the bottom dropped out. While most of the world, including the United States, entered a devastating economic depression at the same time, things were even worse in Germany. Unemployment ran rampant. Millions of men and women no longer had jobs and could not afford to buy the goods that factories were producing. Thus more and more factories closed their doors, and more and more people lost their jobs. Crops rotted in the fields because people in the cities had no money to buy the products. And because farmers could not sell their crops, they too were nearly bankrupt. There seemed to be no end to this downward cycle. Germans became even more bitter and resentful, and many felt they had been unduly punished.

Then along came a man by the name of Adolf Hitler, the leader of the National Socialist German Workers (or Nazi) Party. Hitler promised the Germans that he could solve their problems and bring prosperity back to their nation.

Hitler had been born in Austria, south of Germany. He came from a poor family and had left school at the age of sixteen. Art had been his original career choice, but no school would accept him. He spent his early adult years in poverty, most of which was his own fault. However, this difficult time made a deep impression on him, and he learned to hate those who were rich, well-educated, and successful. And he despised the weak.

During World War I Hitler served in the German Army. When he became a civilian once again, he quickly rose to the top of the Nazi Party and became known for his rousing speeches. Many unemployed workers and ex-soldiers came to hear him, and it was from this group that Hitler formed his storm troopers, bands of armed thugs dressed in brown shirts bearing swastika emblems. With this band of followers, he boldly attempted to seize control of the Bavarian state government in 1923. He was captured, tried for treason, and sent to jail.

Hitler was paroled in December 1924, after serving fourteen months in prison. He soon began to rebuild the Nazi Party. He was a marvelous speaker, and he played on the Germans' resentment over having lost World War I. The German people were desperate for something, almost anything, that would restore their national pride.

Hitler openly expressed hatred for the Communists, accusing them of trying to destroy Germany, and blamed the Jews for Germany's depression. By 1928, it was estimated that he already had 75,000 devoted followers.

Soon the Nazi Party was a force in German politics. In 1932, it won more than a third of the vote in national elections. With no party winning a clear majority, Hitler was able to manipulate the political process and become chancellor of Germany on January 30, 1933. He promptly moved toward dictatorship, setting up a one-man rule that would permit no dissent.

Aware that the German Communist Party was also growing in numbers, Hitler realized that he would have to squash it quickly. When the Reichstag building burned on February 27, 1933, he blamed the fire on the Communists and started a propaganda campaign, spreading rumors that the fire marked the beginning of a Communist revolution. To counter that threat, Hitler was given broad powers, and individual rights were suspended. The truth about the Reichstag fire was not revealed for many years: It had been deliberately set by storm troopers to scare the Germans into putting the Nazis into power.

For fourteen years after the end of World War I, Germans had tried a form of democracy. It had failed. Now the nation, desperately afraid of a Communist takeover, had turned all power over to a fanatic. Not all Germans approved of Hitler's Third Reich government and his Nazi Party. There were some attempts at resistance. But for the most part, Hitler went unchallenged. With a massive propaganda campaign, he was successful in creating an image of himself as a patriot. After years of humiliation and hard times, many Germans were ready to believe him when he told them that they were a "super race" and deserved to rule the world.

*Adolf Hitler addresses a mass meeting of his
followers in Berlin. In 1938, when this picture was
taken, Hitler was in firm control of Germany.*

National pride was boosted further when Berlin became the site of the 1936 Olympic Games. As Germany's capital, the city seemed to be on the rise. But this city, with all its attributes, was soon to experience the devastation of war.

World War II ▪ In September 1939, World War II began when Hitler attacked Poland, putting into action his plan of conquest. He had already taken over Austria and Czechoslovakia without firing a shot. Soon after Poland was conquered, Denmark, Norway, Belgium, Luxembourg, and France all fell to Hitler's invading armies. And in September 1940, he received help when Italy joined forces with Germany. The sounds of marching feet and gunfire were heard again all over Europe. German troops moved south into Yugoslavia, Greece, and North Africa, and Hitler's air force bombed Britain. In the summer of 1941, Germany, in spite of an alliance with the Soviet Union, launched an attack against that country—a move it would later regret. And after Germany's ally Japan attacked Pearl Harbor on December 7, 1941, Hitler also declared war on the United States.

The war dragged on for almost four more years. Hundreds of battles were fought, and millions of men, women, and children were killed. Cities, homes, factories, and buildings were destroyed and lay in ruin. Berlin itself was pounded by Allied bombing raids. Slowly Hitler's forces were beaten back.

By 1945 Allied soldiers had finally reached German soil, and soon they were very close to the capital city. U.S. General Dwight D. Eisenhower, supreme commander of the Allied forces in Europe, advanced from the west, while Soviet troops advanced from the east. Much to the disappointment of American troops, who were held at the Elbe River, the United States permitted the Soviets to enter Berlin first. Later, the United States would receive much criticism for this decision.

On April 16, 1945, the Soviet soldiers began their assault on Berlin. They fought street by street, using harsh methods to secure the city. Hitler, trapped, committed suicide on April 30. And by May 2, Berlin was completely in the hands of the Soviets. Germany formally signed an unconditional surrender on May 8, 1945.

In human lives, the price of the war was astronomical. Total civilian and military deaths were estimated at fifty-five million. Some six million Jews suffered death at the hands of the Nazis simply because they were Jewish, many at extermination camps where they were gassed. Millions of others were brutally treated. Germans also paid a price for the war. Estimates of the German war dead ran as high as six to eight million. And millions of others were injured or lost their homes.

In 1933, Hitler had boasted, "Give me ten years and you will not be able to recognize Germany."[1] Twelve years later, the country was devastated. This time German land was not spared, and Berlin itself paid a particularly heavy price. Air attacks unleashed thousands of tons of explosives on the city, leaving the center of the once-beautiful capital in almost total ruin. Many of its buildings were demolished, and its people were reduced to walking zombies. There was an atmosphere of death everywhere.

Water mains were ruptured, and sewage flooded into canals and lakes that still held dead bodies. Disease struck at an alarming rate. It was almost impossible to get gas for automobiles or electricity for homes. The Soviets destroyed the telephone system and began to strip the industrial plants bare. Herds of cattle were driven off

*Allied bombing and shelling turned vast sections
of Berlin into rubble. The ruins on the left once
housed one of the city's leading newspapers.*

from the farms around the city, subways were deliberately flooded, and there was no police or fire protection.

Other forces soon came crawling out of the rubble. Black markets appeared for items such as food, soap, and cigarettes. Unscrupulous people began purchasing precious articles from destitute Germans at a fraction of their value, and they frequently paid the sellers with worthless currency.

Meanwhile, peace did not come easily. When the Americans finally entered the city, the soldiers were encouraged not to socialize with the German people. They came not as liberators but as conquerors, and they disregarded local customs and barricaded themselves in barbed-wire compounds. Confrontations between Americans and Germans were frequent.

On November 11, 1945, the Soviets dedicated a new monument in Berlin—a sixty-five-foot colossus, flanked by two rearing T-34 battle tanks—near the Brandenburg Gate. The Soviet War Memorial commemorated the Soviet soldiers who had died in the battle to take Berlin. For Berliners, the monument was a daily reminder of defeat. It would be guarded twenty-four hours a day by Soviet soldiers for the next forty-five years.

Occupation ▪ Hitler's military had committed many horrible acts, and the Allies felt strongly that they deserved to be punished. Twenty-one Nazi leaders were indicted for war crimes and went on trial on November 20, 1945, at Nuremberg, where the Nazi Party had once held annual rallies. There, with parades, speeches, and much pageantry, party members used to have their faith and enthusiasm renewed. But now the leaders stood in disgrace, waiting to be judged for what they had done. During the trial, the world became aware of the magnitude of the atrocities the Germans had committed during the war. On October 1, 1946, verdicts were handed down, sentencing twelve Nazi leaders to death. Others received prison terms and fines.

But in spite of the atrocities committed by the German military, the Allied nations were helping the Germans to rebuild their cities and their lives. (They were mindful of what had happened at the end of World War I, when the reparations demanded of Germany had almost brought the country to collapse.) Immediately after the war, millions of CARE packages containing food and other essentials were sent from people in the United States to the Germans to help them survive. And the Allied nations sent equipment and materials to assist in the rebuilding process. Health conditions received top priority. Hospitals had to be rebuilt, and medical equipment obtained. In Berlin, the United States Army helped to eradicate a huge infestation of rats.

Now it was time to bring order back to Germany. But those who had fought to defeat Germany did not agree on the country's future.

Even before the guns of war were silenced, the European Advisory Commission—a group formed by the United States, Britain, and the Soviet Union—had begun to plan for the occupation of Germany. At that time, it was decided that Germany would be divided into three zones, one for each country except France. Later, at a conference held in February 1945 at Yalta, U.S. President Franklin D. Roosevelt and British Prime Minister Winston Churchill were able to convince Joseph Stalin, the Soviet leader, to create a zone for France, which had suffered three invasions and two defeats at the hands of Germany within seventy years. Each of the four zones would be administered by the country occupying the area.

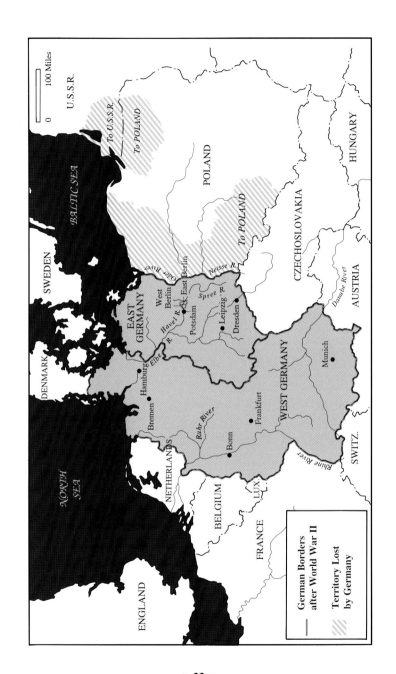

During this time, Roosevelt's health was declining, and Churchill was suffering from a heart condition. The fact that these two world leaders were in such bad physical condition may have played a role in their willingness to give in to many demands by the Soviet Union. One condition was that part of Poland was to be handed over to Russia. And while the Allies agreed that the Germans owed $20 billion for the damage they did during the war, the Russians claimed one half of that amount.

On April 12, 1945, President Roosevelt died and the presidency of the United States passed to Harry Truman. On July 17, the day after the first atomic bomb had been successfully tested at Alamogordo in the New Mexico desert, Truman, Churchill, and Stalin met at Potsdam, near Berlin, at the German crown prince's former summer residence. It was at this meeting that the final decisions were made regarding how Germany should be organized and where its borders would be drawn. The Allies agreed on a border in the west; a temporary line for the east was to be the Oder and western Neisse rivers. (The final eastern boundary was supposed to be determined after the peace settlement, but this didn't happen.) Each occupying country was to make certain that the Germans were not able to build up a military force again.

The city of Berlin, 110 miles inside the eastern zone of the Soviets, became a special area for joint four-power control. Twelve boroughs, including 2,250,000 people living in roughly 188 square miles, were placed in the control of Britain, France, and the United States. This would become the western sector. The Soviets were given eight boroughs in the eastern part of the city, home to 1,100,000 people in 144 square miles. Decisions affect-

Allied leaders pose for reporters in 1945 at Potsdam, where they made the final decisions about Germany's postwar future. From the left are British Prime Minister Winston Churchill, U.S. President Harry S. Truman, and Soviet Premier Joseph Stalin.

ing the city were to be made by the Kommandatura, a council made up of the four occupying powers.

Before the Soviet Red Army officially took control of its zone, there was a last-minute rush of people from east to west. They feared that the Russians would establish a more secure border, one that would be impossible to get through. It was a premonition of things to come.

CHAPTER TWO

AN IRON CURTAIN DESCENDS

The four powers had agreed at Potsdam that Germany would one day be reunited. Then the Germans could vote to choose their government. The division of Germany and of Berlin was to be only a temporary situation. However, it would be forty-four years until reunification would take place.

The division of Germany led to problems. Coal and steel came mostly from the zone given to the British, but this region lacked food. The American and Soviet zones had food but lacked fuel. For practical reasons, then, the Allies began to consider unifying Germany promptly. But strains quickly developed between the four occupying nations.

A Chill in Relations ▪ The Allies were permitted to take whatever steps were necessary to control their zones, including the dismantling of industries. As payment for war damage, the Soviets were allowed to remove from their zone machinery and equipment that wasn't essential to the economy. (The other Allies were also to provide the Soviet Union with machinery from their zones.) The Soviets, who had suffered enormous devastation during the fighting, felt justified in seizing anything they wanted. They shipped to the Soviet Union entire factories, many motor vehicles, railroad cars, and even the rails on which the cars formerly ran. The Soviet zone was almost stripped bare.

Then, in May 1946, General Lucius D. Clay, the American commandant, ordered an end to the dismantling of industries in his zone and stopped further shipments of such items to the Soviets. The British and French followed suit. Efforts in the western zones now focused on helping the German economy recover. This angered the Soviets, who accused the other powers of violating the Potsdam agreements.

The Soviets also had difficulty dealing with President Truman, whose style was much more direct and abrupt than that of President Roosevelt. For their part, the Western Allies mistrusted the Soviet Union under Stalin's grim dictatorship. The resulting chill in relations between the four powers helped lay the groundwork for the Cold War, the period of tension between the Western democracies and the Communist countries that would follow.

Germans in the Soviet zone, meanwhile, were finding that their lives were being rearranged by others. Besides taking over industries, the Soviets took control of large estates and farms, giving the owners a mere portion of what they had formerly held. The ground was being laid for the foundation of a Communist state. The Soviets also began to rearrange the thinking of the East

Germans. They were told that they were victims of Hitler, not his followers. Hitler, they were informed, was an imperialist from the West.

Early in 1946, the German Socialist Unity Party was formed, modeled on the Soviet Communist Party. Activities of other political parties were suppressed. Many East Germans joined this party and began to go to weekly meetings. For many years they had been told that the Germans were the rightful leaders of the world. Now they were being told that they had been lied to, and that international communism, led by the Soviet Union, would take its rightful place.

In the Western zones, the Allies encouraged democratic self-government. Various political parties formed, and elections were held for local governments in 1946 and for state legislatures in 1947. Land and industry remained in private hands. Thus Germany was caught in a strange situation: a democratic, capitalistic system in the West, and a Communist one in the East.

Competing Systems ▪ Capitalism is based on privately owned businesses that produce the goods people want or need. Production and prices are determined largely by the rules of supply and demand that operate in a free market. Under communism, the national government owns the principal means of production—factories, mines, transportation systems, farms. The government sets production quotas and prices. Housing is state owned; in fact, private ownership of property is banned.

In Communist theory, this government control is called socialism and is viewed as a transitional phase from capitalism to true communism—an ideal society, distinguished by common ownership of the means of production, a superabundance of goods, and distribution that would be fair and practically free. In practice, Communist governments have never moved beyond the stage of state control. And they have ruthlessly suppressed dissent, establishing totalitarian regimes that sought to control all aspects of life.

In the years immediately after World War II, the Soviet Union set up Communist regimes throughout Eastern Europe, in the countries from which they had driven the Germans. Increasingly, these countries were cut off from the West. In describing the regimes that the U.S.S.R. had forced on countries and its attempt to extend its rule, on March 5, 1946, Winston Churchill declared: "An iron curtain has descended across the Continent." Of the Soviets, he said, "I am convinced that there is nothing they admire so much as strength and nothing for which they have less respect than for military weakness."[1] The military and political barrier behind which Eastern Europe was placed thus became known in the West as the Iron Curtain.

A year after Churchill's speech, on March 11, 1947, President Truman announced that the United States would support free peoples who were resisting attempted subjugation by armed minorities or by outside pressures. He clearly meant Communists. The policy, known as the Truman Doctrine, included the dispatch of $400 million in aid and civilian and military advisers to help Greece and Turkey maintain their governments in the face of Communist pressures.

Soon after, U.S. Secretary of State George C. Marshall announced a plan for the United States to provide friendly aid to get Europe back on its feet economically. This plan was dubbed the Marshall Plan, and Truman referred to it as "America's answer to the challenge facing the free world."[2]

It had been hoped by many that the United Nations, formed soon after World War II, would ensure peace, not only in Germany, but throughout the world. But by now it was becoming obvious that the capitalist United States and the Communist Soviet Union, which had co-operated to defeat Germany, were not compatible. Their competing ideologies and their struggle for worldwide influence helped feed the rivalry between them.

Nowhere was this more clear than in Germany, with two very different forms of government developing within its borders. Now it remained to be seen whether the capitalists or the Communists would dominate, or if the two systems could actually coexist. And the city of Berlin, deep inside the Soviet zone but under four-power control, found itself in a unique predicament.

The Attempt to Strangle Berlin ▪ In 1948, with tension between the Soviets and the Western Allies mounting, the Soviets attempted to force the Allies from the city. The events began in February, when the Soviets began to tighten travel restrictions between East and West Berlin. Access to West Berlin was already limited; Allied officials, for example, were restricted to one highway and one rail line between western Germany and West Berlin. Now, while government officials, foreigners, and approved workers still traveled back and forth, the Soviets established more rigid restrictions and demanded permits, frequently causing endless delays. When the Soviets stopped parcel post delivery, goods began piling up in warehouses.

On June 21, 1948, the three Western powers decided to unite their zones into a single unit, with the goal of forming a West German state the following year. In addition, they announced a decision to issue a new

West German currency. This raised the question of what currency would be used in Berlin, since the city would be economically tied to the East or the West depending on which it used.

Unable to get the Soviets to agree to a single occupation currency for the entire city, and unwilling to use a Soviet-issued currency, the Western powers announced that West German marks would be used in Berlin. Angered, the Soviets introduced a currency of their own into the city on June 23. The next day, they began to impose a blockade on Berlin.

Demanding that all Western troops leave the city, the Soviets shut off all land access to the western sectors. Roads and railways were blocked. Barges could no longer use the canals, and the power lines that carried electricity from East Berlin to the western sectors were turned off. The Soviets were trying to bring Berlin to its knees.

Cut off from the world, with all eighty entry ports sealed, the western sectors could probably have kept going for no more than six weeks. The only alternative appeared to be to give in to the Soviets and remove all American, British, and French troops from Berlin. The situation looked hopeless. But the Allied nations did not want to leave Berlin—none of them trusted the Soviet Union.

The only way to go was up. And, on June 26, 1948, planes from all over the world were employed to begin an airlift to fly needed food and supplies to the Berliners. The Soviets attempted to frighten away the Allied planes. One Soviet plane, trying to tighten the blockade, fired on a British plane as it attempted to land in Berlin. Both planes crashed, killing all aboard. But the airlift continued.

*During the 1948–49 airlift, children climb trees
to watch for incoming planes loaded with supplies.*

Soon a stream of 5,000 flights a week were bringing relief to the western sectors. Pilots reported that they could see planes lined up in front of and behind them as they attempted to get into the city. The skies over Berlin were filled with planes almost twenty-four hours a day, and planes were landing just three minutes apart. Outgoing planes carried thousands of refugees out of the city.

Goods were sometimes dropped from the air by parachute to save landing time. Since West Berliners were in desperate need of fuel for heating their homes, attempts were made to drop bags of coal from the planes this way. But when the coal was crushed on landing into nothing more than dust piles, it was decided to fly it directly into the city.

Internally, the city was in turmoil. Communist demonstrators drove the elected city assembly from power, and the administration was divided between East and West. But the conduct of the Berliners in the western zones during the blockade was heroic. In spite of the hardships that they lived under and the constant Soviet threats, their courage came through. They imposed on themselves a rationing system that was stricter than that required by the military, and somehow they managed to survive.

By early 1949, the Soviets, realizing that they had failed in their attempt to force the Allies out, were looking for a way to save face. Finally, they agreed to end the blockade. On May 11, 1949, when the Soviets turned the electrical power back on, the lights came on all over Berlin for the first time in more than a year. And by the next day, the blockade was over.

The Allied forces had mustered their strength and come to the rescue of the city. Berliners were soon able to get fresh fruit, vegetables, and clothing. But they also wanted an end to their unbearable political situation. The four powers agreed to expand trade between the sectors and to allow the movement of people and goods. They also agreed to administer the four sectors in such a way as to make life more normal for the Germans. But the city remained divided. And despite their participation in this agreement, the Soviets still made it extremely difficult for anything or anyone to move in and out of the western sectors.

Creation of NATO ▪ Many people recognize the beginning of the Berlin blockade as the start of the Cold War because it was at this moment that the Soviets indicated that they were prepared to risk direct confrontation with the West, confrontation that could possibly lead to war. It was then that most people in the West began to think of the Soviets as adversaries. The Germans had ceased being the enemy, and the Soviets took their place. The Western armies in Berlin were no longer thought of as occupying forces. Instead, they represented protection from the Soviet Union.

The blockade also confirmed American leadership in the West. The United States had been thinking of pulling out of Berlin, but the blockade changed that. The Soviets, with their willingness to put an entire city in jeopardy with the blockade, had demonstrated to the Americans that the Europeans were in danger. Perhaps if the Soviets hadn't taken this step when they did, events would have turned out dramatically different: The United States might have withdrawn, and Berlin might have been absorbed by the Communist regime of East Germany.

Instead, largely to prevent further aggression by the Soviet Union, the North Atlantic Treaty Organization (NATO) was created on April 4, 1949. The charter members included the United States, Canada, Denmark,

Iceland, Norway, Italy, Portugal, Britain, France, Belgium, the Netherlands, and Luxembourg. Greece and Turkey joined in 1952, West Germany in 1955, and Spain in 1982. This was the first time that the United States participated in a defensive alliance during peacetime. The countries banded together to collectively provide national security—Article 5 of the NATO charter states, "The parties shall agree that an armed attack against one or more of them . . . shall be considered an attack against all of them."[3] But NATO also promoted political, social, and economic ties among the members.

Two Governments ▪ The blockade also speeded the desire of the Western powers to establish an internal government for the western zones of occupation. The Western-occupied territories in Germany adopted a constitution on May 23, 1949, establishing the Federal Republic of Germany (FRG), with a multiparty system. And on August 14, 1949, the West Germans voted in national elections for the first time since 1932, with seventy-eight percent of eligible voters participating. The new Federal Republic government removed most restrictions from private enterprises and reformed tax laws. Direct government involvement in the economy was kept to a bare minimum, although the government played a major role by promoting international trade.

On September 15, 1949, Konrad Adenauer, seventy-three years old, was elected the first chancellor of West Germany, a post he would hold until 1963. The city of Bonn, on the Rhine River, was the new capital of the FRG—a temporary capital, until Germany could be unified and Berlin could once again take that position. One half of Germany was healing itself.

The new West German leaders felt that they were not in a position to do much about divided Berlin. Their prime concerns were establishing West Germany as a member of the Western alliance and building trade. Besides, since Berlin was still occupied by Western troops, they felt the Berliners were under the protection of the Allies. But Berlin, despite the lifting of the blockade, was still considered a hostage of sorts because it was completely surrounded by the Soviet zone.

The German Democratic Republic (GDR), or East Germany, was born on October 7, 1949. It was dominated by the Communist Socialist Unity Party (SED). East Berlin became its capital, and Wilhelm Pieck was chosen as the first president. But true power was in the hands of Communist leader Walter Ulbricht. Ulbricht, the son of a tailor, had built a network of loyal followers by rewarding those who backed him with desirable posts. And his close ties with the Soviet Union gave him the opportunity to call on the Soviets for favors.

On paper, the constitution of East Germany was similar to that of West Germany. The authority to rule was to lie in the parliament, the People's Chamber. All citizens over eighteen were given the right to vote. But elections in East Germany lost all meaning because the government chose the candidates and voters merely came out to demonstrate their "approval." Participation was often less than voluntary, as many workers were marched to the voting places. The election results were guaranteed. In fact, all important decisions were made by the government, and no dissent was allowed.

With the two governments and their officials in place, the curtain was ready to go up on a difficult forty-year struggle.

CHAPTER THREE

DIVIDED CITY

By the 1950s, West Berlin was on its way to a sweeping economic recovery, a recovery that reflected the renewal of West Germany itself. The United States government poured large amounts of money into the city to help in its rebirth. In addition, a steady flow of refugees from the East provided the West with a labor supply to replace the workers who had been lost in the war. Business flourished. Industries found a marketplace for their products among a population that had been deprived of consumer goods for many years. Demand for goods pushed wages up rapidly. Thousands of new housing units were built to replace those that had been destroyed or damaged in the war, creating additional jobs. Cultural activities also resumed. West Berliners had the opportunity to go to movies, see plays, and hear concerts. Life was good in West Berlin.

*A modern bell tower, rising beside the ruins
of the Kaiser Wilhelm Memorial Church, became
a symbol of West Berlin's rebirth.*

If life was good in West Berlin, in East Berlin things were going from bad to worse. Prices of food were soaring, and living conditions were poor. Workers barely made enough money to survive, and there was an extreme housing shortage. Some construction was undertaken, but materials and workmanship were often so shoddy that occupants found their buildings crumbling beneath them within a few short months.

Coupled with economic hardship was a hardship of another kind: the loss of intellectual freedom. Suppose you went to the library for a book about another country with a different form of government, and were told that you had no right to that book and were in fact forbidden to read it. Or imagine that your local newspaper printed only news approved by the government of your town and never carried information about what was going on in foreign lands. You would know little other than what your government wanted you to know.

For centuries, governments have been able to control their people by keeping information out of the hands of the public and banning freedom of expression. Hitler knew this; in 1933 he had his storm troopers create bonfires with books the Nazis disapproved of. Since those who have access to information also have power, the East German and Soviet Communists, like Hitler, had to control what East Germans were told.

At first, the East Germans had permitted a wide variety of plays, books, and other forms of expression. But gradually tight controls were placed on all cultural activities. Newspapers in East Berlin and throughout East Germany restricted news about what was going on in the rest of the world; those publishers that did not soon found it impossible to buy paper to print on. Citizens could not get Western books or magazines, or any information considered hostile to the Communist government. The shelves in the libraries contained only approved books. The East German government also controlled the radio stations, and they filled the airwaves with propaganda. And artists and writers were no longer free to produce their own works. They were told what they could do. Anyone who violated these rules risked imprisonment. East Germans lost something that Americans take for granted, their intellectual freedom.

The Border Crossers ▪ As the Communist government sought to impose its control on East Germany, West Berlin was a thorn in its side—a glittering capitalist showcase sitting in the middle of Communist territory. The border between the two parts of the city was marked merely with a white line painted on the asphalt. Although it was patrolled, motorists from the West could cross after a routine scrutiny of identity papers. East Berliners had to pass through a more rigorous inspection, but it was legal to cross—and many did.

To make decent wages, tens of thousands of East Berliners crossed the border each day to work at jobs in West Berlin, returning to their homes in the East at night. Potsdamer Platz, where the American, British, and Soviet sectors in Berlin converged, was the point where many of these border crossers, or *Grenzgänger,* lined up each day to go to work. Some took one of the trains that still linked the city, while others simply walked or rode their bicycles across the border, passing through the arches of the Brandenburg Gate or one of the other border crossings.

The crossers received forty percent of their pay in West German marks, which were worth four times the East German marks. As a result, they could live much better than their counterparts who worked in East Berlin and had no access to the currency from the West. They also had access to the cultural and political freedom of the West, a fact that made the East German government increasingly uncomfortable. Despite the fact that crossing the border was legal, protest letters began to appear in the government-controlled newspapers. The writers called the border crossers "parasites" and demanded that they be stopped. Although the letter-writing campaign clearly seemed to be orchestrated by the government, for the time being the workers continued to cross the border, returning every night to their homes in the East with the West marks jingling in their pockets.

Even more serious, from the East German government's point of view, was a flood of refugees who used Berlin as a gateway to the West. As life began to get harder and harder in East Germany, while at the same time the West Germans were enjoying economic security, skilled workers and professionals in the East started fleeing their homeland. The border between East and West Germany was rigorously patrolled to prevent this. But it was fairly simple for East Germans to go to East Berlin and then cross into the western part of the city. They could remain there or, with the help of the West German government, travel on to the West.

In the early 1950s, the number of refugees grew by leaps and bounds. There were not enough houses in West Berlin to accommodate them, and many had to be temporarily housed in warehouses. All types of skilled workers, students, and professionals, including doctors and nurses, were fleeing the East. The East German work force was being depleted and, although the birthrate was increasing, the population was declining. The East German government felt that something had to be done to stop the flood.

The 1953 Uprising ▪ Those East Germans who remained behind were increasingly dissatisfied. Industry was in the hands of incompetent people, and the laborers had lost all pride in their work. There was little hope for the future, and no incentive to do better.

In June 1953, the dissatisfaction erupted in a revolt. Crowds gathered in Alexanderplatz, East Berlin's main square, and the streets of East Berlin were scenes of mass demonstrations by workers, some of which turned violent. From Berlin, revolt spread like wildfire across East Germany. Rioters, sometimes with the help of local police, opened jails filled with political prisoners. East Germans wanted their lives changed—something that their government had no intention of permitting.

The revolt caught the East German leaders off guard, and they were not prepared to deal with the situation. Before too long, they were forced to call on the Soviet Union for help. The Soviets responded by sending in armed units. While Communist leader Ulbricht was whisked away to safety in a Soviet tank, the blood of many East Berliners ran in the streets. In all, more than 240 East Berliners and some 800 East Germans were killed. Many more were arrested and executed or imprisoned by the authorities after the revolt was put down.

The uprising marked the first time that the Soviets had used armed force to control people in a neighboring country. It would not be the last.

Firm Control ▪ A few months before the uprising, on March 5, 1953, Soviet leader Joseph Stalin had died. Nikita Khrushchev became the new Soviet leader. At one time, Khrushchev had been an extremely underrated man within the Soviet government. But with Stalin's death he emerged as the most powerful figure in the Soviet Union, and he consolidated his control within three years.

East Berlin demonstrators hurl bricks at a Soviet tank during the 1953 uprising.

At the Brandenburg Gate, flag-waving marchers demand free elections.

A man who was often difficult for people in the West to understand, Khrushchev was semieducated but very shrewd. He managed to make some improvements in the Soviet economy, in particular improving a terrible housing shortage. He was also responsible for bringing about a mild thaw in the Cold War. And he began to demolish the myths that had been built around Joseph Stalin, revealing the brutality of his predecessor.

With changes taking place in the Soviet Union, there were hopes that the situation in East Germany would improve. Some people speculated that Walter Ulbricht might be replaced. But it soon became clear that Khrushchev did not intend to make any changes in the leadership of East Germany; at least, not yet. And as long as Khrushchev remained in charge and favored Ulbricht, nothing was likely to change in East Berlin.

Ulbricht, with his balding head, wispy gray mustache and goatee, steel-rimmed glasses, and paunchy stomach, was often a target for Western cartoonists. He was an unemotional man, with simple tastes and a passion for physical fitness. Ulbricht was a firm believer in the strict form of Communist rule practiced by Stalin. A former cabinetmaker, he had trained for political office in Moscow; and the older he grew, the more intolerant he became. He was never popular with the East Germans, but he had built his following carefully, rewarding those who were faithful to him.

To all appearances, the Soviets were pleased with Ulbricht, and they were not going to meddle with him. When, in 1958, Ulbricht disposed of Communist Party members he felt were not loyal to him, he did so without any interference from the Soviet Union.

Through the 1950s, Germany and especially Berlin continued to be a flash point of tension between East and West. There were repeated efforts to ease the situation. In 1954, a conference of the four Allied powers was held in Berlin to discuss the problems in Germany. But the conference produced no solutions. The 1955 Geneva Conference, hailed as a major step toward problem solving, also had little effect. The Allied powers reasserted their intention to unite Germany after free elections, but no progress was made toward reaching that goal.

In fact, East and West Germany were growing further apart. West Germany joined NATO in May 1955, aligning itself firmly with the West. The step was taken after a long debate on rearming Germany that had begun with the outbreak of the Korean War in 1950. Until North Korea, backed by the Soviet Union, invaded South Korea, communism had been viewed mainly as a political threat. Most people hadn't believed that the Communist powers would actually use armed force to extend their influence. But now the fear of war between the United States and the Soviet Union grew stronger.

The Western powers debated how West Germany could help in defense plans, to prevent the Soviet Union from taking control of more territory in Europe. Many people were unwilling to let West Germany rearm, even though they wanted additional protection from the Soviet Union. Fear of Germany was still deeply implanted in the minds of the people who had suffered at the hands of the Nazis, and many considered the Germans politically immature and lacking understanding of their past mistakes.

Finally, West Germany was permitted to recruit troops based on the so-called Spofford Plan. Under this plan, Germany could have only one armed military person for every five in other European units. In addition,

Germans had to operate their army without benefit of a general staff or heavy armaments. Rather than a true national army, the German forces were to be tied to NATO. The Allied nations hoped that these restrictions would prevent Germany from becoming a military threat once again. But many West Germans were not eager to be armed. The slogan ''include me out'' was adopted to show their reluctance to be part of any army.

One week after a rearmed West Germany entered NATO, on May 14, 1955, the Communist countries formed their own defensive alliance, the Warsaw Pact. And if anyone doubted the Soviet intention to keep control over Eastern Europe, those doubts ended in 1956, when Soviet troops crushed a revolt in Hungary.

Khrushchev's Ultimatum ▪ In November 1958, Khrushchev precipitated the next crisis over Berlin by calling on the Western powers to withdraw from the city. The call soon became an ultimatum: The Soviets gave the Western powers six months to leave Berlin. If they did not, the Soviets said, they would conclude a peace treaty with East Germany that would formally end World War II—and any justification for Allied garrisons.

Berliners panicked. They felt that their security and freedom would be threatened if the Allies moved out, for they feared the motives of the Soviet Union. The Western allies, however, soundly rejected Khrushchev's proposal and ignored his ultimatum, keeping their troops in Berlin. The Soviets backed down.

The confrontation did lead to a new round of four-power talks. But these talks, along with several rounds that followed and summit meetings between U.S. and Soviet leaders, brought no change. Berlin remained divided.

*Soviet Premier Nikita Khrushchev (left) and
U.S. President John F. Kennedy (right) in
Vienna, Austria, in 1961. Khrushchev demanded
that the West withdraw from Berlin.*

In early June 1961, the new president of the United States, John F. Kennedy, met with Khrushchev in Vienna, Austria. Once again, the question of divided Germany was on the agenda. And once again, the Soviet leader issued an ultimatum: The Western powers were to remove their garrisons from Berlin within six months and recognize the "reality" of East Germany. (The West had never formally recognized the East German government, insisting that Germany should be unified and that the East was simply the Soviet zone of occupation.) Berlin itself would become a "free city," and the Western powers would have access to it only if the East Germans allowed them in.

Kennedy answered that the United States would not allow the Communists to drive the Western allies out of Berlin. He indicated that America intended to maintain security both in the city and in West Germany. But this time, the Soviet ultimatum was followed by a chilling threat: If the West did not comply, Khrushchev implied, the Soviet Union was prepared to fight a nuclear war.

CHAPTER FOUR

THE WALL OF SHAME

Even as tension mounted between the United States and the Soviet Union, Berlin continued to be a channel for people fleeing to the West. And their numbers continued to grow. In the first seven months of 1961, more than 200,000 people left the eastern zone of Berlin in search of freedom.

The East German government felt that it had to do something to keep from losing all its workers. But what? In the West, there was growing speculation that the Berlin border would be restricted.

At a press conference soon after the U.S.-Soviet summit, on June 15, 1961, a reporter asked Walter Ulbricht about his plans for the frontier. Ulbricht replied, "I take your question to mean that there are people in West Germany who would like us to mobilize the building workers of the German Democratic Republic's capital to build a wall. I am not aware of any such intention. Our building workers are busy erecting new houses. Nobody wants a wall.''[1]

Until then, no mention had been made of the possibility of a barrier between East and West Berlin. Most people dismissed the remark. But Ulbricht was in fact planning to close the border, and a wall figured prominently in his design to keep East Germans from fleeing to the West.

The East German leader was in a strong position to act, having driven from the government anyone who was not absolutely loyal to him. With the death of Wilhelm Pieck in 1961, the East German People's Chamber selected Ulbricht as its president. And in September 1961, the government gave him additional powers. Ulbricht now had supreme power in East Germany, and he called the shots in East Berlin. Moreover, in the atmosphere of confrontation between the United States and the Soviet Union, he was able to convince Khrushchev that a wall had to be built. A wall would both shut people in and annex East Berlin to Communist East Germany. What the Soviets had not received in the original agreement with the other Allied powers would now be taken with concrete and barbed wire.

Up to the very last minute, however, Ulbricht kept the plan secret. He talked about establishing reliable safeguards and controls to protect East Berliners from ''subversive activities'' by West Berliners. But he guaranteed his people that there would be no military conflict, and he never mentioned that he intended to build a wall.

Still, there were signs that something was afoot. It was suddenly announced that 45,000 recruits had ''volunteered'' to serve with the Vopos, the East German People's Police, and the Grepos, the border guards.

(Everyone knew that there were no "volunteers"—the government had merely pressured people to join the ranks.) Well-armed Soviet soldiers began to replace East German soldiers near the border. Then the government started stockpiling coils of barbed wire, as well as thousands of concrete poles.

Now the East Germans had the tools to build a wall, and the guards needed to ensure it would be built.

August 13 ▪ At first, it was a Sunday night like any other. Most East Berliners were in bed before midnight. Others lingered with their friends in small cafés; some were enjoying themselves in dance halls. Still others were on their way home from visiting friends and loved ones who lived in the West. Few people, if any, were aware that a long column of Soviet jeeps was headed for Berlin. Little did anyone realize that fifteen minutes past midnight on August 13, 1961, was zero hour—the hour that Ulbricht, with the help of his protégé Erich Honecker, would start to build the Wall.

One group of travelers, who were on a train heading toward West Berlin at about that time, were startled when the train abruptly came to a halt several miles from the border. They were told that the train was going no farther and that they would have to finish their journey by foot. Suddenly, as they were passing through the stately columns of the Brandenburg Gate, the lights went out and they were plunged into darkness. Almost from nowhere, East German militia carrying rifles and machine guns filled the streets.

As these and other travelers hurriedly stumbled home in the dark, the plan to close the border proceeded. By 2 A.M. armored cars had appeared outside the Soviet Embassy. All traffic had been stopped, and all trains had ceased running. Telephone lines between East and West had been cut. Streets connecting the two sections had been blocked. And almost silently, Soviet troops had ringed the city, while ten thousand East German soldiers lined up behind them.

All was ready for the workmen to begin their task. Using jackhammers, they started to dig up the streets that had linked the city's sectors. Concrete posts were set, and barbed wire was strung along the border. East German tanks and soldiers, along with Vopos carrying snub-nosed automatic guns, protected the workers. Some of the East German guards took off their cartridge belts so that they could help sink concrete posts.

Potsdamer Platz was one of the first areas to be sliced in two. Here and at other sites, crowds began to gather on the West Berlin side. Tension mounted, and at times it appeared that the crowds would surge across the street in a mass attack on the East Germans. A few brave young West German men even tried desperately to rip the barbed wire down. But East German soldiers, who were posted every five yards along the barrier, drove them back with fixed bayonets. An old water-cooled Maxim machine gun was wheeled into the center of Potsdamer Platz and aimed at the agitated crowd. High-pressure streams of water were also used to discourage interference with the construction. Machine guns were mounted on top of the Brandenburg Gate, the main crossing point from West to East Berlin.

West German police arrived to keep the crowds away and avoid more trouble, but the construction was allowed to proceed. Reporters from various countries also began to appear at the scene. Av Westin, a field producer for CBS-TV, was in Berlin making a documentary on the escalating crisis in the city when he heard a

Opposite page: Behind barbed wire and plasterboard screens, the Wall goes up in August 1961. The Reichstag building is in the background. Above: An East German soldier carries barbed wire to the border.

rumor that something strange was happening at the Brandenburg Gate. Within minutes, he had his camera crew at the site, where they shot some amazing 16-millimeter footage of the barrier being erected. (At that time, photographs and films had to be flown by plane to the United States, so Americans did not see the events until two days later. Compared with the way news in the 1990s can be moved by satellite, the 1961 method seems like slow motion.)

The crowds that formed on the East Berlin side of the barrier were quieter, and people were kept well back from the construction. West Berliners who had been trying to get home after visiting friends and family in the East on that August Sunday had been delayed, but they were eventually allowed through. East Berliners who hoped to enter the western sector were simply turned away by the guards.

Construction of the barrier continued through the day. Blue-shirted boys and girls of the East German Free German Youth Movement arrived at the site to present the workers and the guards with bouquets of flowers, soft drinks, and pastries. They appeared well-rehearsed, bursting into patriotic chants. Some young Communists, eager to demonstrate their commitment to the party, climbed to the rooftops of homes and toppled aerials that might be bringing in television news from the West. Eventually Ulbricht himself showed up and gave a speech, telling the audience that the East Germans had struck a mighty blow against the capitalists.

Later, the Western powers were accused of knowing in advance that the Wall would be built. These charges were based on the fact that some American families were moved out of East Berlin just before the Wall went up. However, American military staff denied the accusations and maintained that they were as surprised as everyone else.

In fact, while evidence had pointed to some form of border restriction, few people had thought it would happen so swiftly or take this form. The East Germans had managed to keep their scheme secret by allowing only a tiny group of dedicated followers to know about it. Secrecy was maintained right up to August 13. One group of people who might have exposed the plan—the printers who were hired to make signs that announced that the borders were closed—were locked up in their plants, with their families, until after midnight.

By nightfall on August 13—a day that became known as "barbed-wire Sunday"—the barrier was in place. Later, Willy Brandt, the mayor of West Berlin and a man who would emerge as one of the strongest voices in West Germany, would say that the cold concrete posts that split Berlin were rammed into the heart of Germany.

The World Reacts ▪ A few days after the barrier went up, Brandt spoke for nearly an hour to a crowd that overflowed the square before the Town Hall. He said that he wanted representatives from every nation to come to Berlin and view the barbed wire. When he called for more than oral support from other nations, the crowd broke into enthusiastic applause.

Brandt wanted the Western Allies to send patrols to the border, to bolster the morale of the West Berliners by at least showing the flag and some muscle. His request was turned down. The countries of the West condemned the closing of the border, but they were not prepared to take action against it.

The United States did send some 1,500 troops to

Separated from friends and family, West Berliners
peer over the concrete blocks into East Berlin.

strengthen its West Berlin garrison. U.S. Vice President Lyndon B. Johnson, in Berlin to welcome the troops, delivered a stirring speech to approximately 500,000 people and promised that the United States and the West Berliners would see the crisis through together. As the troops paraded down the Kurfürstendamm, one of West Berlin's main avenues, the Johnson visit reached a high point. Not since the days of the blockade had any statesman aroused such warmhearted feelings as this Texan from America. But even with the reinforcements, the U.S. troops in West Berlin were vastly outnumbered by Soviet and East German troops. There was little they could do but to stand and watch the Wall go up.

The New York Times declared Johnson's visit a symbol that would make clear to Khrushchev that "the West was under an obligation to prevent with all necessary means any further encroachments on the frontiers of freedom."[2] But it quickly became clear that the Western nations were united in urging negotiations as the only way out of the impasse. The use of any military force was widely held to be unnecessary and dangerous.

The Western leader closest to the scene, West German Chancellor Konrad Adenauer, did practically nothing to intervene. While he called the building of the Wall a violation of Allied pacts and pledged that the Allies would take countermeasures, he also cautioned against worsening the crisis.

Other nations also stood by. The Canadian government took the position that the NATO allies were obligated to fight only if West Berlin were attacked. Newspapers in Britain warned against cutting off trade with East Germany or placing economic sanctions on the Soviet Union. The *London Daily Herald* stated, "Closing of the means of escape is no reason for the postponement of negotiations over Berlin. Rather it makes much more imperative the acceleration of preparations for a conference."[3]

Willy Brandt was among many West Berliners who were deeply disappointed that the United States did not respond more quickly and vigorously to the building of the Wall and who felt abandoned by a trusted ally. Brandt said, "The curtain went up and the stage was empty."[4] While he remained friends with President Kennedy, America's lack of action kindled anti-American sentiment in West Germany and came in for some criticism at home. Edward R. Murrow, the famous American commentator and newsman, said, "If Washington continues to react as it has until now, U.S. policy in Berlin faces a fiasco. The mood of the population is miserable. If Washington doesn't act immediately, we are threatened with a political catastrophe."[5]

But Nikita Khrushchev said, "The West will stand there like dumb sheep."[6] And so they did.

Officially, the Communist position was that East Germany had acted to protect its own interests. One of the propaganda techniques used by the East Germans to justify their actions was to print statements, supposedly made by East Berlin citizens, praising the closing of the border. One farmer was quoted as saying, "We farmers still have confidence in our government. Everything it has done benefits us and the cause of peace." A locomotive repairman was reported to have said, "Naturally we must tolerate many small inconveniences in connection with the border closing, but these are a small sacrifice in contrast to the great sacrifice for war."[7]

The Power of the Wall ▪ The barbed-wire barrier was only the first step in sealing off West Berlin. Over the following weeks and months, the wire would be replaced with a massive wall built of concrete blocks and slabs. Tracks for streetcars and railroads were bent back, and ditches were dug in any place that a car or truck could possibly navigate.

The Berlin Wall zigzagged just on the eastern side of the lines established in 1945, cutting through parks, factories, and homes. It divided families and destroyed friendships, slicing through the middle of the community. Relatives and friends could no longer meet, although they could sometimes see one another from across the border. West Berlin, more than ever, became an island in East Germany.

In many places the Wall was built right down the middle of city streets. This meant that there were houses very close to it on each side. On the East side, troops began commandeering houses and turning people out. Windows on the first floor were boarded up. The East Germans were creating a no-man's-land up to 300 yards wide on their side of the Wall; such a space would be difficult for people to run across without being seen by the guards. Eventually a second concrete barrier was constructed on the East Berlin side, to make doubly sure that no one would get across. Thus the Wall was actually two barriers, with a wide deserted strip between.

The Wall was about 28 miles long where it cut through the center of the city, and it curved around over 70 miles to divide West Berlin from East Germany. It ranged in height from nine to twelve feet. Thirty thousand troops manned 193 watchtowers, 208 bunkers, and other reinforced positions. They were assisted by guard dogs and batteries of floodlights, alarms, minefields, and automatically triggered guns. The East German soldiers always patrolled in pairs, to prevent their own from running away. Guards had permission to shoot on sight. On the East Berlin side, the Wall was painted white so that the soldiers could readily see the outline of anyone trying to escape. It was against this backdrop that hundreds would be shot during the next twenty-eight years as they tried to scramble over the barriers to freedom.

A handful of crossing points, or checkpoints, permitted officials and those with special permission to pass through the Wall. All were heavily guarded. To prevent cars or trucks from gaining momentum and crashing through the checkpoints, the East Germans embedded concrete obstacles in the roadways.

Checkpoint Charlie, the main crossing point for the American sector of West Berlin, was only 680 feet west of the Brandenburg Gate. It was here, on October 27, 1961, a gray and chilly day, that the tension over the Wall came close to erupting into military conflict. The issue that provoked the incident was one of principle: The United States insisted that its officials did not have to show their passports to East German guards when crossing into East Berlin, while the East Germans insisted that they did. The United States sent tanks, military jeeps, and soldiers to Checkpoint Charlie. The jeeps began to escort U.S. officials across the border to ensure that they would not be challenged.

In response, Soviet tanks rolled into East Berlin. Soon ten Soviet tanks faced ten American Patton tanks less than a hundred feet away. But after sixteen tense hours, shortly after 10:30 A.M. the next day, the Soviets backed off. After that, American officials were instructed to stay out of East Berlin, so that they would not risk another confrontation.

The tank confrontation, dramatic though it was, contributed nothing to solving the basic problem of the

*U.S. tanks (foreground) face Soviet tanks
at Checkpoint Charlie in October 1961.*

Wall. Could the building of the Wall have been prevented? Many thought that the United States, through weakness and uncertainty, had allowed itself to be pushed back by communism. But others argued that the building of the Wall could have been prevented only at the risk of starting another war—a price that the world was not prepared to pay. Looking back, it is difficult to say if the Western Allies would have made the same decisions had they known how long the Wall would stand or how many lives would be damaged or destroyed before it would be torn down. But even if they had known, a decision to wreak the devastation of war on so many people would have been extremely tough for the Allies to make.

For the time being, then, the Wall stood firm. Its foreboding appearance served as a warning of death to those who might want to challenge its power to gain their freedom.

CHAPTER FIVE

ESCAPE TO THE WEST

As the Wall grew higher and higher, the desire of many East Berliners to escape confinement also grew. The chances of anyone actually getting over the Wall were dismally poor, but those who wanted to be free continued to try.

During the first several hours after the border was closed on August 13, 1961, a few people managed to bribe their way through with cigarettes or money. Some even tried to drive their cars through the barbed wire. But most were turned back. After that, the greatest number of escape attempts were made in the first year or so after the closing of the border, while the Wall was still being built. Some escapes were attempted on the spur of the moment, while others took months of planning. Either way, ingenious people managed to go over, under, through, or around the ominous Wall. Still others, whose mangled and bullet-ridden bodies were found along the barrier, bore grim evidence of how desperately they wanted to be free.

Jumping to Freedom ▪ One of the first escape methods that East Berliners used was to jump out of windows in apartment houses that were directly beside the Wall, landing in the western zone. When East German police boarded up the first-floor windows in the buildings, people used the second-floor windows. When the second-floor windows were sealed, escape attempts were made from third- and fourth-floor windows.

West Berlin firemen held nets and tried to catch the people as they leaped or swung across the open space with ropes. Some people managed successful jumps from as high as several stories; others fell to their deaths. During one twelve-hour period thirteen adults and several small children managed to reach safety by jumping out of their apartment windows onto mattresses that they had previously tossed out.

In some cases, the West Berlin police managed to keep the Vopos occupied by tossing tear gas shells at them while people made it to safety from a window. But eventually East German police barricaded all the windows and evicted more than 2,000 families who lived in houses alongside the Wall. The area became deserted.

Climbing the Wall ▪ One of the most dangerous methods of escape was to climb the Wall. At first, people could escape by throwing a looped rope over the top and hoping it would either catch on something solid or be caught by a helpful West Berliner. Then the East banned the sale of rope and twine that was strong enough to hold a human being. But attempts to climb the Wall continued. Some people even tried to vault over the top

*East Berlin police try to pull an escaping woman back
into a building, while West Germans gather to help her.
The woman finally escaped, landing safely in a net.*

using stilts. One ingenious butcher strapped bacon, hams, sausage, and veal roasts around his body and hurled himself over the barbed wire. His wares acted as a protective shield, absorbing bullets.

Most people were not so fortunate. In November 1961, thirty people tried to climb the Wall, but only nine were successful. The rest retreated under heavy East German police fire.

A particularly tragic attempt was made in August 1962 by two young East German construction workers, Peter Fechter and Helmut Kulbeik. They had spotted an empty building near the crossing to the American zone, managed to enter without being seen, and found one window that was not completely boarded up.

Two days later, they returned and managed to rip off the barbed wire and boards that partly blocked the window. Then Peter, tall and slim, dropped out of the window first, followed by Helmut, who was short and stocky. They raced over the wasteland and met their first obstacle—more barbed wire. Slipping through, they dropped onto a sandy roadway that ran between the barriers. Ahead of them stood the ominous Wall.

The young men ran forward. Helmut was the first to climb, tearing and tugging at more barbed wire as he reached the top. As he was about to swing over, he realized that Peter was still at the base, looking terrified. A border guard stood just a short distance away.

Then the firing began. As bullets pierced his body, Peter struggled to climb the Wall. Miraculously, he reached the top. But he was unable to lift his body over the barbed wire, and for a minute he remained crouched on the Wall, unable to go farther. Then he toppled back on the wrong side and lay there bleeding.

West Berliners who had seen Peter on top of the

Wall rushed to the area, but they could do nothing to save him. The West Berlin police and the U.S. guards at Checkpoint Charlie nearby could not help because they were forbidden to set foot in the East. The East German guards did not dare to approach Peter—they feared they would be shot by the Western police—but they kept their rifles aimed at the young man. Newspaper reporters and photographers joined the crowd that was gathering at the scene. Some people even tried to climb the Wall, but the border guards threw tear gas into the crowd.

Tension was mounting. The West Berliners shouted at the East German guards, growing more angry by the minute, and demanded that the American guards carry Peter to safety. One young U.S. lieutenant, who did not want to violate his orders, made the mistake of saying to the crowd, "Sorry, but this isn't our problem." [1]

When Peter had lain on his side for over fifty minutes, the East border police finally approached and carried him away on a stretcher. He died, the fiftieth victim of the Wall.

After Peter's death, riots broke out in West Berlin. Stones, bottles, and bits of scrap metal were thrown at the East German border guards, who tossed smoke and tear gas canisters back at the angry mob. The crowd also became increasingly angry with the Americans who had not gone to Peter's aid. The next night and for five days after the incident, there were demonstrations in the western section of Berlin. The Peter Fechter incident negatively influenced the attitudes that many Berliners had about the Americans.

About two years later, Michael Maier, a twenty-one-year-old jockey, was involved in another dramatic escape. As he climbed on top of the Wall, the Vopos opened fire. He took five bullets in the chest and arms.

Maier raised himself in one last attempt to get over the barbed wire, but his knees crumpled and he toppled back, falling at the foot of the Wall on the East Berlin side.

Five U.S. soldiers raced upstairs in a West Berlin apartment building that overlooked the Wall and saw that the border guards were grabbing Maier and pulling him back into their zone. The Americans aimed their rifles at the guards, ordering them to leave the man alone.

After several tense seconds, the border guards released Maier and walked away. Although wounded, he began to crawl back to the Wall. West Berlin firemen then climbed onto the Wall, threw him a rope, and pulled him to safety.

Such dramatic attempts became less and less frequent as time went on. When the Wall was completed, climbing it was nearly impossible. Those who managed to get across the first barrier and past the guards, alarms, and mines in front of the Wall were faced with a tall barrier that was topped by slick-surfaced concrete tubing. As they struggled to get a grip on the tubing and hoist themselves over, they were targets for the guards' automatic rifles.

Through the Wall ▪ Challenging the formidable Wall head-on was no easy task. But in 1961, before the barrier was completely in place, some daring attempts were made. One group of young men managed to steal a bus and tried to crash through the East German roadblocks. One yard from freedom, guards opened fire with pistols and carbines. The Vopos joined the fight with their machine guns. The bus and the young men inside were riddled with bullets.

Three other young men took a Soviet car and put false Soviet plates on it. They then put stars, cut out of cardboard and painted gold, on their raincoats and piled maps and official-looking papers on the car seats. With a young girl who hoped to escape with them hidden under a blanket, they brazenly drove to the checkpoint. Astoundingly, they were waved through to the other side.

The driver of a low-slung sports car, along with his fiancée and her mother, managed to drive right under one of the barrier gates, ducking to dodge the bullets. After this incident, the East Germans put a staggered maze of gates at the checkpoints, so that no one else could escape in this embarrassing manner.

One East German was accused of murdering an East Berlin taxi driver in October 1961 in order to use the vehicle to escape. He was sentenced to death. (He was also accused of having been a spy for the United States, a charge that was never substantiated.)

In December 1961, a train engineer stowed his family and some of his friends on a train and drove it right through the last stop in East Berlin and into the West. The East Germans then tore up the tracks near the border, closing off this escape route.

A month after the train escape, twenty-eight people, one of the largest groups to escape at one time, were able to flee East Berlin. The refugees slipped through the barrier and into the French sector without attracting the attention of the East German guards. They included ten men and eighteen women, one of whom was paralyzed and was carried across. One young man cut a hole in the barbed wire and ran across first to notify the West Berlin police. Meanwhile, the other members of the group hid in the underbrush. When the young man finally signaled with a flashlight that the way was clear, the rest of the party rushed across.

On April 29, 1963, four men crashed through the

Wall in an East German army truck. They were fired on by East German border guards, but none was hit. The truck got stuck in the Wall, two thirds of it jutting into West Berlin. The four were in the cab of the truck and thus able to escape unhurt under fire. Two weeks earlier, a young East German had also plowed through the barricade, in an armored car he had stolen in the army garage where he worked as a civilian mechanic. He was hit by East German gunfire but survived.

Other people used trickery to get through the Wall. An East Berlin woman brought flowers to the guards and then, as she handed the bouquet over, turned and bolted for the border. A guard ran after her, shouting for her to stop—and escaped to the West himself.

Under the Wall ▪ The first underground escape route was the sewers of Berlin. During 1961, a number of people fled by groping through a network of sewer lines that ran under the border. The route was filthy and very hazardous—the pipes were quite narrow in places. But the refugees managed to make their way through the dark, smelly caverns. Eventually, however, the East German police located all the sewer manholes and cemented them shut. (It has been charged that some people were trapped in the sewers when this was done.)

In January 1962, Western newspapers reported that over a period of several weeks, twenty-eight people had managed to escape to the West through a tunnel. East German police blocked the tunnel immediately after the article was published. This caused a furor in West Berlin, where people claimed that publication of the story had shut off the route for other people who planned to use the tunnel. However, United Press International, the wire service that had put out the story, said it had re-

Above: Even East German soldiers escaped. This soldier hopped the barbed wire barrier soon after the border was closed. Below: When East German officials found this tunnel, they brought in excavators to dig it up.

ported the incident only after East German police had discovered the tunnel and occupied the house that was its starting point.

In any case, there were soon more tunnels. An elderly East German tailor and his wife made their way to the western zone on October 7, 1962, through a tunnel that led from the cellar beneath their tailor shop to the basement of a closed-up restaurant on the western side. Five West Berliners went through the tunnel to the East to help get them out. One was shot by East German guards armed with machine guns. When West Berlin ambulance drivers wanted to go through the gate to help him, they were refused; the East Germans said that they would render aid. It was not known whether the young man survived the ordeal. Later, East German guards wrecked the tunnel with pneumatic drills.

One group of people discovered a clever way to escape. Starting at a mausoleum in a cemetery bordering the Wall, they dug a tunnel to the West. "Mourners" would then file into the mausoleum but never come out. The route worked well until a woman in one of the groups took her baby into the mausoleum but left the baby's carriage outside. Guards spotted the carriage sitting outside the tomb, became suspicious, and found the tunnel. They destroyed it with a demolition charge.

Tunnels were being built all over town. As soon as one was discovered, another one was started. Harry Seidle, a well-known tunneler and a hero to the East Berliners (as well as a former cycling champion), helped hundreds of people escape before he was arrested and sentenced to life at hard labor on December 29, 1962. Max Thomas, 81, led a group of twelve East Berliners, most of them in their 50s, 60s, and 70s, through a tunnel that started behind his chicken coop. This senior citizen was successful in guiding the group to freedom.

However, tunneling also created a new but contemptible enterprise. Some unscrupulous tunnel builders began to charge each escapee large sums of money, while others would agree to help people escape and then betray them to the East German police.

Escape by Water ▪ Berlin's canals and rivers were still open to navigation, and at first they provided a perfect escape route. One group of people, pretending to be picnickers, managed to use a little excursion boat to float down a canal to safety. A couple placed their baby in a floatable tub and swam to freedom as quietly as they could beside the sleeping child.

Another group, which included several people who did not know how to swim, used inflated tubes to cross the Teltow Canal just two days after the border was closed. They made so much noise that it was believed that the guards had simply pretended not to see them. But the next day, searchlights and machine guns were installed at different points along the canal and its branches. And a motorboat, equipped with a searchlight, began to patrol the waters.

On May 25, 1962, a nine-year-old boy swam the canal under gunfire. The boy suffered wounds but survived. But several days later, a man was shot and killed as he tried to use the same escape route. And on June 5, 1962, another man was shot and killed as he attempted to swim to freedom across the Spree River. A few days later, a group of thirteen people seized the 500-ton excursion boat *Friedrich Wolf*. They raced the vessel through machine-gun fire and rammed it into an embankment on the West Berlin side of the Spree River.

Still others reached West Berlin from East German territory outside the city, by swimming the Havel River. But the banks of the river, which were patrolled constantly, were soon dotted with crosses commemorating the deaths of more than seventy people who had been shot while trying to swim across.

Through the Air ▪ One creative couple decided to try to escape East Berlin by building a hot-air balloon. They managed to gather up pieces of fabric and used a forty-year-old treadle-operated sewing machine to make their balloon. On the first attempt, the balloon was not airtight and would not rise. On the second attempt, the balloon carried the couple and their two children up into the sky. The winds were strong and the balloon kept spinning around in circles. Finally it landed—much to their dismay, in East Germany. They then made a third balloon, much larger than the other two and able to hold two families, a total of eight people. One Sunday, when the winds were favorable, the families climbed into the balloon and cut the ropes that had held it to the ground. This time they made it.

Escape by air was more common outside the city, in remote rural areas where people could fly into West Germany without attracting attention. In the early 1970s, Barry Meeker, an American helicopter pilot, flew three missions into East Germany to bring refugees out. Flying at treetop level to avoid radar, he revved up his speed and roared past the guard towers along the border. He managed to get several people out before he was wounded on his third and final mission. (Meeker was killed in 1982, in a helicopter accident in Colorado.)

The Wall Grows Stronger ▪ At noon on August 13, 1962, traffic stopped in West Berlin for what was to have been three minutes of silence to mark the first anniversary of the closing of the border. Motorists blew their horns instead. Later that afternoon, Soviet vehicles carrying soldiers were assaulted by stone-throwing West Berlin crowds. Frustrated West Berliners then held a demonstration at the Wall. Carrying crosses and torches, the marchers, about 4,000 strong, hurled taunts, stones, and beer bottles across the barricade into East Berlin. East German guards responded by tossing tear gas canisters. Automobiles roared through the area with horns blowing. West Berlin police arrived and tossed smoke bombs back at the East Germans until they retreated. The West Berlin police finally dispelled the crowd and closed off the area within two blocks of the Wall.

Meanwhile, to discourage escape attempts, well-publicized trials were held in East Berlin. The sentences handed down were extremely harsh—four people were sentenced to death and eighteen to life imprisonment in the Wall's first two years.

Even the threat of death and prison sentences did not stop determined people from trying to escape, however. During the first two years that the Wall divided Berlin, it was beaten 16,500 times. But it also took its share of human life. Sixty-eight people were shot to death, and 618 more were fired at. The escape attempts, especially those that ended tragically, contributed to the anger and frustration created by the Wall.

CHAPTER SIX

"LET THEM COME TO BERLIN"

Construction of the Wall was completed in 1963, and West Berlin was sealed off. In June of that year, President John F. Kennedy flew into the city, and Berliners went wild.

Torn paper, rice, and flowers showered from windows and rooftops as the president's limousine made its way through the city. People stood on top of automobiles and buses, clung to lampposts, and climbed trees to catch sight of the U.S. president, who was riding with West German Chancellor Adenauer and West Berlin Mayor Willy Brandt. When he drove past the Soviet War Memorial, even the Red Army sentries snapped to attention. And as his car wound around the streets near the Wall, several East Berliners bravely waved.

President Kennedy returned the waves of the people and smiled broadly, appearing to enjoy his reception thoroughly. No American leader had ever been greeted

*Cheering crowds line the streets of West Berlin
as President John F. Kennedy's motorcade passes
in 1963. Standing in the car are (from left) the
president, West Berlin Mayor Willy Brandt, and
West German Chancellor Konrad Adenauer.*

with such joy and obvious popularity. Later, thousands of people jammed Rudolph-Wilde-Platz in West Berlin to hear him speak.

"All free men, wherever they may be, are citizens of Berlin. Therefore, as a free man, I take pride in the words: *Ich bin ein Berliner!* (I am a Berliner)," Kennedy told the crowd, which roared in approval. "There are many people in the world who really don't understand, or say they don't, what is the great issue between the free world and the Communist world. *Lasst sie nach Berlin kommen* (Let them come to Berlin)." [1]

Ironically, as Kennedy flew out of Berlin, Khrushchev flew in to celebrate Ulbricht's seventieth birthday. But there was no contest when it came to determining which leader the German people admired the most. Kennedy won hands down.

Just a few months later, however, Berliners were stunned when they heard the news of Kennedy's assassination on November 22, 1963. People began to fill the streets to make certain that they had heard the news correctly. Kennedy had represented hope and faith to Berliners, and now he was gone. Berliners, both East and West, placed candles in their windows in memory of the president. The Vopos saw the candles burning brightly in East Berlin homes, but they did nothing.

Several days later, in tribute, the square where Kennedy had made his speech was renamed John-F.-Kennedy Platz. Willy Brandt said, "The Americans have lost the president of whom it was believed by so many that he would be able to lead us firmly along the road to a just peace and a better life in this world. But we in Berlin grieve because we have lost our friend." [2]

Lyndon Johnson assumed the presidency of the United States, and life went on. In Berlin, the Wall still stood. On the fourth anniversary of its building, in 1965, West Berlin observed an hour of silence. Wreaths were laid all along the western side of the Wall.

For the next twenty-four years, the city would remain split. And Berliners learned to live with the Wall, despite the sorrow and anger that it caused. Children of the same national heritage grew up under radically different systems and developed completely different viewpoints. Many had little idea of what life was really like on the other side.

Life in Divided Berlin ▪ As time went on, West Germany developed one of the strongest economies in Europe. West Berlin shared in its prosperity. An influx of foreign workers in the 1970s, including many Turks, provided labor for the city's growing industries. The bombing damage of World War II had been virtually erased. Cafés were thriving, music was everywhere, and tourists were welcome.

West Berliners, especially students, showed themselves to be independent spirits who spoke their minds freely. Large and sometimes unruly demonstrations were common—to protest conditions in universities, U.S. racial problems and involvement in the Vietnam War, and the stationing of NATO nuclear weapons on West German soil.

In contrast to the western zone, East Berlin seemed grim. Despite a facade of new public buildings, the city was still run-down. Visitors noted the dilapidated streetcars filled with unsmiling passengers, the lack of flowers, the absence of small inviting shops. Life in East Berlin was not easy. State subsidies kept rents and prices low, and employment was guaranteed. But wages, which were likewise controlled by the government, were also low; and the state-run industries were inefficient. With no prospect of improving their lives, workers had little incentive to work. The quality of the goods available was terrible. East German razor blades could be used only once or twice before they had to be thrown away. Local shampoo was latherless. Shoes were hard and uncomfortable throughout their brief lives. Although East Germany developed one of the stronger economies in the Communist world, life there could not rival the life that East Berliners could glimpse over the Wall.

By 1968, the East German constitution had been changed to eliminate or diminish rights that had once been allowed, such as the right to emigrate and the right to strike. The East German government also managed to strictly control information and expression. The Ministry for State Security (Stasi)—the secret police—maintained networks of informers and kept files on thousands of citizens. Anyone suspected of disagreeing with the government risked being carried off to jail. Needless to say, students were not allowed to demonstrate for any viewpoint other than that held by the government.

Some of the worst effects of the economic hardship and political repression in the East were felt by families. Families were split in two by the Wall—brothers were separated from sisters, parents and grandparents from children and grandchildren. Typical was the story of an East Berlin building engineer and his wife. Over a period of a dozen years, three of the couple's children—a son and two daughters—escaped to the West by hiding in the trunks of cars that smuggled them through checkpoints. The children found better lives, but their parents were cut off from them.

Still, the East Berlin government couldn't prevent its citizens from receiving West German television. And there were direct contacts with the West, too. Limited telephone service between the two parts of the city was restored in 1971. (Until then, calls had to be routed through West Germany.) Tourists traveled to East Berlin, although they were seldom permitted to mingle with the people there.

The East and West German governments also reached an agreement under which West Germans could obtain permits to visit relatives in the East. Passes were first issued at Christmas in 1963. From then on, the number of people allowed into East Berlin under this arrangement—and the fees the East Germans charged for the permits—varied with the state of relations between East and West.

In 1975, East Germany signed the Helsinki Final Accord, an international pact that, among other things, guaranteed human rights. Supposedly, this would give tens of thousands of people the right to leave East Germany and go to other lands. However, only a few thousand were permitted to leave. Most East Germans still had to risk bullets if they attempted to flee.

There were contacts of another kind, too. Berlin, the point where the West rubbed shoulders with the Communist world, was a center of espionage. Both East and West based networks of spies in Berlin. Some performed their work out of loyalty to their ideology, while others did it for money or other rewards.

Typical was the story of a West German police officer, Hans Weiss, who was arrested in November 1965 when it was discovered that he was a key man in the East German espionage network in West Berlin. Weiss had a desk job in the main office of the West Berlin police and thus had access to reports of anti-Communist investigations. He had been able to warn Communist agents when the police were after them, so that they could go underground or flee. Weiss, aged fifty-nine, was arrested less than a month before he was to retire.

Berlin also became the site where the East and West exchanged captured spies. Many of the exchanges took place on the Glienicke Bridge, which links East Germany and West Berlin. One of the most famous exchanges on this bridge took place on February 11, 1986, when the Soviet Jewish dissident Anatoly B. Shcharansky was freed in an East-West exchange that involved nine people accused or convicted of espionage. Shcharansky's supporters maintained that he had been targeted by the Kremlin because of his outspoken criticism of Moscow's policies, especially toward Soviet Jews. His release came after eight years of imprisonment and forced labor.

Political Changes ▪ The years between the building of the Wall and the 1980s also saw changes in politics and leaders, both in the West and the Communist world.

West Berlin continued to hold the status of both a city and a state of West Germany. But it was not fully a part of West Germany because four Allied powers remained in occupation. The Western allies would not sign a treaty that would formally end their occupation because to do so they would have to recognize East Germany as a separate country, with Berlin as its capital. However, by the end of 1973, sixty-eight countries had established full diplomatic relations with East Germany. Others would follow suit. Soon even the United States was dealing with East Germany.

By this time, new leaders had come to power. In West Germany, Willy Brandt had become chancellor in 1969. He worked hard to improve relations with the East, hoping to gain the reunification of Germany. On August 12, 1970, West Germany and the Soviet Union signed a treaty renouncing the use of force to settle disputes between them. In 1971, Brandt's steadfast defense of freedom won him the Nobel Peace Prize. He served as chancellor until 1974, when it was discovered that one of his personal aides was an East German spy. The resulting scandal forced his resignation, and Helmut Schmidt assumed the post.

In East Germany, meanwhile, Walter Ulbricht dominated the scene through the 1960s. But Ulbricht fell from power in May 1971, at the age of seventy-eight. He was permitted a dignified exit but was clearly out of favor; when he died in 1973, no Soviet officials attended his funeral.

Erich Honecker, the man who had carried out Ulbricht's order to build the Wall, was his replacement. The son of a coal miner, he had joined the Communist youth organization at age ten. At seventeen he had joined the party, and at nineteen he had become an official of its youth organization. From then on he had risen through the ranks of the party as Ulbricht's protégé.

Honecker was very different from Ulbricht. A pale man who wore thick, horn-rimmed glasses, he was far more subtle and more inclined to face the reality of situations. At first, he was vastly underestimated. But as he gained power, it became clear that he would be no less firm a ruler than his predecessor.

In the Soviet Union, too, the major players changed. In 1964 Khrushchev was removed as first secretary of the Communist Party. He was replaced by a man who had helped overthrow him, Leonid Brezhnev. By this time, the Communist world was growing increasingly restless. Like the East Germans, people in the Soviet

Union and Eastern Europe faced shortages of food and fuel. The government-controlled economic system simply wasn't working, and the repressive atmosphere was suffocating. But under Brezhnev, nothing changed.

East and West ▪ The level of tension between the Communist world and the Western democracies fluctuated through the 1960s and 1970s. Periods of confrontation were followed by periods of lessening tension, or détente. Berlin was not the flash point that it had been in the early 1960s. More often, the focus was elsewhere— in Vietnam, where the United States became embroiled in a long and bitter war, and in other parts of the world.

One area of confrontation continued to be Eastern Europe. In 1968, the government of Czechoslovakia began to take steps toward reform. The Soviet response was to invade. An estimated 200,000 troops from five Warsaw Pact nations crossed the borders of Czechoslovakia on August 20, 1968. By early the next day, they had taken control of the whole of Czechoslovakia. New, hard-line leaders were installed, and Soviet troops stayed behind to ensure that they would remain in power.

To justify the invasion of Czechoslovakia, Brezhnev asserted that it was the right and duty of Communist countries to render what he called fraternal assistance against counterrevolution. In other words, the Soviet government would use force whenever it was needed to keep Communist rulers in power. This policy became known as the Brezhnev Doctrine.

While the United States did not intervene in Czechoslovakia, the incident raised anew the threat of war between the superpowers—the same threat that had once been raised by their confrontation in Berlin. There were repeated efforts to reach arms control agreements that would lessen the threat of nuclear war. For the most part, they met with only limited success. However, the Strategic Arms Limitation Talks (SALT), which began in 1969, ended in 1972 with two agreements. One was a limit on deployment of antiballistic missiles, and the second set limits on numbers of intercontinental ballistic missiles and submarine-launched missiles.

With the two sides negotiating in a spirit of détente, the Cold War seemed to be waning. But the ideological rivalry between the superpowers was not at an end. The Vietnam War continued into the 1970s, and the Soviet Union was charged with interfering in Angola, Ethiopia, and Yemen. In 1978, the Brezhnev Doctrine was applied again when Soviet troops invaded Afghanistan to prop up a pro-Soviet regime.

Although a second SALT agreement was signed by President Carter and Brezhnev in Vienna in June 1979, this treaty was never approved by the United States Senate. Once again, tension between the two countries grew. By the end of 1979, intermediate-range rockets (which could almost reach Moscow) and ground-launched cruise missiles (low-flying jet drones that are difficult to pick up on radar) were scheduled to be placed in West Germany. This was in response to Soviet placement of SS-20 mobile missiles in Eastern Europe. The Soviet missiles had the potential to reach any target in Europe and could overshadow the West's nuclear weapons.

Germany, once again, seemed a likely stage for World War III. And the German people began to express grave concern. The shifting political climate brought massive anti-nuclear demonstrations. It also gave strength to the Green Party, which took pro-environment and pro-disarmament stands and opposed nuclear energy as well as nuclear weapons. And a vocal minority in West Ger-

*Demonstrators in West Berlin protest a plan to place
intermediate-range missiles in West Germany.*

many began voicing anti-American feelings. They did not like the fact that Germany was caught between the two superpowers, and they wanted to be in charge of their own destiny.

Into the 1980s ▪ The 1980s brought a new round of changes in leadership. Ronald Reagan took office as U.S. president in 1981 and began a massive arms buildup, coupled with renewed opposition to the Soviet Union. Helmut Kohl became chancellor of West Germany in October 1982 and helped lead his country out of a recession. By the mid-1980s, it had emerged as one of the richest countries in the world.

Winds of change were also beginning to stir in the Communist world. In 1980, the independent union Solidarity became the spearhead for a movement by the Polish people to try to rid themselves of Communist domination. Late in 1981, however, the Polish government, under pressure from Moscow, banned Solidarity and imposed martial law.

Although the Polish movement was crushed, it was a sign of things to come. But true change, when it arrived, would come from an unexpected direction—from the Soviet Union itself. The change began in 1985, when Mikhail Gorbachev was chosen first secretary of the Soviet Communist Party. The world didn't know it then, but the event signaled a new chapter in history.

Glasnost and Perestroika ▪ Gorbachev began by talking about the need for the Soviet people to learn to work in new ways. The Soviet economy, like Communist economies elsewhere, had continued to deteriorate through the 1970s and early 1980s. Now it was near collapse. Gorbachev introduced two policies that, he said, would bring new life to the country and turn the economy around.

The first was *glasnost,* a term that came to mean openness, especially in public affairs. After years of repression, the Soviet people were told that they could criticize their government and thereby help shape their own destiny. Gorbachev also promised that strict emigration controls would be relaxed and that his government would observe international standards of human rights. *Glasnost* was intended to help the economy by encouraging people to expose corruption and to recognize failures. But the policy also led to a rebirth of Soviet culture. New literary magazines began to appear on the scene, and the theater and the arts began to thrive once again. The Soviet people also began to learn more about their own country and the outside world.

Gorbachev's second policy was *perestroika,* or restructuring. It encompassed a range of economic, political, and social reforms. Taken together, these changes would vastly reduce the central government control of the economy, even permitting a measure of private enterprise. And they would involve Soviet citizens more directly in their government, bringing a measure of democracy to the country.

Gorbachev's policies also brought changes in relations with the West. Strategic Arms Reduction Talks (START), on hold since 1983, resumed in 1985. Within a year, the two sides were also making progress toward an agreement that would remove intermediate-range missiles from Europe.

Not all Soviets welcomed *glasnost* and *perestroika.* Gorbachev proceeded very slowly, anxious not to provoke a reaction from traditionalists. But he said, ''What is at stake is the country's future, the future of socialism. We have no right to permit *perestroika* to founder on the rocks of dogmatism and conservatism, on anyone's prejudices and personal ambitions."[3]

In East Germany, the government watched the developments in the Soviet Union with unease. While some East European governments began to echo the Soviet leader's calls for reform, East Germany hung back. Its economy was not much stronger than those of many other Communist countries. But the government had no intention of relaxing its control—to do so would surely mean that East Germans would once again flood to the West.

On August 13, 1986, East Germany commemorated the twenty-fifth anniversary of the Berlin Wall with a parade of 8,000 troops along Karl-Marx-Allee in East Berlin. Erich Honecker reviewed the event. In a speech, he referred to the building of the Wall as a historic deed that had laid the foundations for sustained prosperity in East Germany.

The three Allied powers issued a statement that called the parade a clear-cut violation of the demilitarized status of Berlin. West Berliners marked the occasion differently—by laying wreaths along the Wall in memory of those killed attempting to cross. Chancellor Helmut Kohl spoke at the Reichstag building, which had housed the pre-World War II German parliament. He said, "As long as there is a wall, barbed wire, and orders to shoot, there can be no talk of normality in Germany."[4]

The next year, President Reagan visited Berlin and, in a speech to thousands of West Berliners, challenged Gorbachev to tear down the Wall. In fact, the winds of change that were stirring in the Soviet Union would soon reach divided Berlin.

CHAPTER SEVEN

THE FALL OF THE WALL

Gorbachev's policies set the stage for even more remarkable events. As the world began to see where this Soviet leader was going, it eagerly followed. In fact, it jumped ahead of him. When Gorbachev said openly that people would no longer be persecuted or confined for their political beliefs, his words sparked hope in many Eastern European countries. And, as the economic picture grew bleaker in one Communist country after another, the torch of democracy began to blaze brighter.

In 1988, as Poland slipped into an economic crisis, workers again raised the Solidarity banner. This time, instead of cracking down, the government allowed the union to regain its legal status. In 1989, Poland's freest elections in half a century led to a new government that included Communists and Solidarity members.

Hungary, too, was taking steps toward greater economic and political freedom. Far from trying to stop such changes, the Soviet Union seemed to encourage them. During 1989, Gorbachev visited several Western European countries, including West Germany. In early July, speaking to the Council of Europe at a meeting in France, he implied that the Soviet Union had no right to interfere in the affairs of its neighbors. Less than four months later, he went further, explicitly renouncing the Brezhnev Doctrine. (Soviet foreign ministry spokesman Gennadi I. Gerasimov even joked about the policy shift, telling reporters: "You know the Frank Sinatra song 'My Way'? Hungary and Poland are doing it their way. We now have the Sinatra Doctrine.")[1]

But even before Gorbachev's formal renunciation of the right to use force to keep Communist governments in power, the events that would destroy the Berlin Wall had been set in motion.

Cracks in the Wall ▪ In East Germany, the economy was rapidly falling apart. Industries were antiquated, and production was extremely low. Housing conditions were terrible, food was in short supply, and worker morale was low. And when East Germans compared their state with that of West Germans, they were not happy.

Then, in mid-1989, Hungary became the first Soviet-bloc country to open its borders with the West. East Germans, who were permitted to travel to Communist-ruled states such as Hungary, suddenly found an escape route. From Hungary, they could travel freely to neutral Austria and then to West Germany, which guaranteed them citizenship. By October 4, when the East German government closed its borders to stop the flood, more than 40,000 East Germans had fled to the West through Hungary and through Poland and Czechoslovakia, where they took refuge in Western embassies.

An East German scales a fence to reach the West German embassy in Prague, Czechoslovakia. Thousands of similar escapes took place in 1989.

At the same time, opposition to the government mounted within East Germany. With the threat of Soviet military intervention removed, a movement for democracy began to take hold. In September 1989, East Germans formed a group called New Forum to challenge the Communist political monopoly, and they began to hold weekly demonstrations in the city of Leipzig. Protesters were beaten and arrested. But the demonstrations swelled as more and more people turned out to demand democratic reforms.

Erich Honecker issued a written order for security forces in Leipzig to be prepared to fire on pro-democracy demonstrators. However, other officials countermanded the order. And on October 18, the East German Communists ousted Honecker as their leader. (Within a very short time, in response to a public outcry over revelations of widespread party and government corruption, a number of other East German Communist leaders would also resign. It was revealed that Honecker and his cronies had enjoyed luxurious life-styles, while engaging in embezzling, influence-peddling, bribe-taking, and currency speculation. By some estimates, they had hidden more than $54 billion in Swiss bank accounts.)

Honecker's replacement, Egon Krenz, promised a moderate course. Protestors who had been arrested were freed, and police were ordered not to interfere with peaceful demonstrations. Krenz also promised to talk with opposition groups, including New Forum. But he found himself riding a tiger, unable to keep pace with the events that were rapidly changing his country. (Krenz, too, would resign before the end of the year, to be replaced by Hans Modrow.)

East Germany opened its border again with Czechoslovakia on November 1, 1989, and two days later

Czechoslovakia followed Hungary's example and opened its borders. Once again, thousands of East Germans rushed to the West. Meanwhile, the pro-democracy movement continued to hold huge demonstrations. In early November, more than 500,000 people took part in a peaceful march that ended in East Berlin's Alexanderplatz. In addition, the largest unauthorized demonstration since the worker revolt of 1953 took place in Leipzig.

In a desperate effort to keep control, the East German government promised sweeping reforms. East Berlin party chief Günther Schabowski vowed that the regime would give all political forces in the country a right to compete in elections. Schabowski told his people, "The Wall will not come down immediately, but we will make it invisible from our side."[2]

Then, on the evening of November 9, the government abruptly announced that the border between East and West Germany—and between East and West Berlin—would be opened. Permission to travel or emigrate would be granted quickly and without preconditions, government officials said. The move was a gamble to stem the stream of refugees to the West. If East Germans were allowed to cross into West Germany or West Berlin freely, perhaps they would not emigrate.

"Gates Open!" ▪ In East Berlin, people began to go to the Wall to see if what they had heard was true. It was. Within two hours of the announcement, the trickle of people had turned into jubilant crowds. By midnight, thousands of East Berliners were walking, biking, or driving to crossing points in the Wall and entering the western half of the city—something that, just a few hours earlier, they could only dream of.

At Checkpoint Charlie, the place where U.S. and Soviet tanks had faced off while the infamous Wall was

Thousands of East Berliners march on November 4,
1989, to press the government for reform.

being erected, long lines of cars and people moved into West Berlin unimpeded. Berliners were shouting, "Gates open! Gates open!" and "The Wall is gone!" Some exuberant Germans even scampered to the top of the Wall, now that all fear of being shot was gone.

As East Berliners drove their cars down the splendid Kurfürstendamm, West Berlin's equivalent of New York's Fifth Avenue, their enthusiasm grew. They had dreamed of entering the western zone for years, and now they were seeing their dreams come true. It was an emotional time—many had difficulty describing how they felt. One woman exclaimed, as she viewed the shop windows of West Berlin, "There is so much color, so much light." "It's incredible," "The eighth wonder of the world!" "I never believed I would be able to do this!" were other remarks. Of the West Berliners, one East German student said, "It's amazing how warmly we were greeted. We were applauded. They cried. They were just as happy as we were."[3] A blind man, guided by a seeing-eye dog, remarked, "I just wanted to smell the air of a free Berlin."[4]

East German guards, who hours before would have shot anyone trying to escape, now posed happily as people snapped pictures of the scene. "The East German soldiers don't know what to do now," said one West Berliner. "They behave a bit crazy tonight, so calm and so quiet."[5] One man rushed across the border carrying a copy of a newspaper that proclaimed, in an enormous headline, "Berlin is Berlin Again!" The guards, who previously would have confiscated such material, merely reached out eagerly to see the newspaper.

The celebrations continued all through the night and into the morning. People began to dance on top of the Wall. Others blew trumpets, embraced, and laughed while tears streamed down their faces. The ringing of chisels

ALLIE
CHECKPOINT

West Berliners clap as East Berliners pour through Checkpoint Charlie the day after the opening of the border.

An East Berlin border guard hands a flower back to West Berliners sitting atop the Wall.

and hammers could be heard as people began to chip away at the once-impregnable barrier.

The next day more crossings were opened, including the Glienicke Bridge, the site of many East-West spy exchanges. A hundred thousand East Berliners inundated the western zone. Among them was an East Berlin man who had borrowed three books from the American Memorial Library in West Berlin the day before the Wall went up. Now, twenty-eight years later, he returned the books—in excellent condition. (Presumably, no late-book fines were imposed.) The visitors eagerly lined up at banks to receive sixty dollars provided by the West German government. Aware that their bonus money wouldn't buy too much, many East Berliners decided not to spend it right away.

The Next Step ▪ In December, with the last travel restrictions set to end, East and West German leaders stood side by side at a ceremony to mark the reopening of the Brandenburg Gate in Berlin. The Wall was open, and people were free to go and come across the frontier. Many Germans began to look toward the next logical step: reunification of their country. Freedom of movement gave the Germans hope that someday the two Germanys would be one.

Reunification would be no simple matter. The Germans had to unscramble two separate governments, sort out two different currency systems, coordinate telephone and rail systems, and understand the entirely different philosophies that had guided East and West. They had to handle the closing of antiquated East German industries and find employment for people who lost their jobs as a result.

Some of the difficulty could be gauged by the problems that East German immigrants were encountering in adapting to life in the West. While the West had been enjoying a healthy economy and a high standard of living, the East Germans had lived much more modestly. The average monthly income in West Germany was more than 3,000 West German marks, while in East Germany it was less than 1,300 East German marks. East Germans had lived without many of the conveniences that most West Germans took for granted. For instance, only seven percent of East Germans had telephones in their homes, compared with ninety-eight percent of West Germans. And while ninety-seven percent of West Germans owned cars, only fifty-two percent of East Germans did. Prices for food and other goods were also radically different in the two Germanys. One month's rent for an East German was 75 marks, while West Germans had to pay 411 marks. But West Germans could buy a color TV for only 1,500 marks, while East Germans had to put out 4,900 marks.

Many of the East German immigrants began to sense rejection as they attempted to build new lives in Berlin and in cities throughout West Germany. West Berlin employers complained that the people from the East had a different work ethic—low motivation and little understanding of the spirit of teamwork. The people from the East, however, charged that the Western employers had unrealistic expectations and looked down on them.

There were also different points of view on how the East and West Germans came to have such different lots in life. West German workers maintained that they had worked hard for what they had and deserved their well-off life-style. Many East Germans, however, believed that the West Germans had just been lucky. They felt that the West owed them a great deal.

Thus some of the joy both sides experienced in the emotional pulling down of the Wall began to decrease as these two different cultures mingled. Some Germans urged caution, and a few maintained that East and West Germany should remain separate. They feared that they had been separated for such a long period of time and had existed under such completely different ideologies that it would never be possible to come together as one nation.

But the West German government favored prompt reunification. A massive influx of refugees in 1989 had created problems for West Germany. During 1989, it was estimated that more than 843,000 refugees arrived. Several hundred thousand new citizens suddenly needed jobs, housing, and services—no easy task for the West. Moreover, the West Germans were concerned that, with travel restrictions lifted, the influx would continue. Only reunification would put East and West Germans on an equal footing and end the stream of immigrants.

In East Germany, too, feeling ran strongly in favor of reunification. The mass migration of Easterners was affecting both the East and the West. West Germany continued to prosper. In the East, however, the loss of thousands of people hurt the already poor economy.

Late in 1989, Chancellor Kohl outlined a ten-point plan to produce a confederation of East and West Germany. It began with aid for East Germany. After a freely elected government was installed in the East, the two countries would move toward economic and political union.

The Soviet Union reacted coolly to Kohl's proposals. It was one thing to renounce the use of force in Eastern Europe. It was quite another to allow East Germany, one of the key members of the Warsaw Pact, to simply disappear by merging with the West.

But even this was to change in 1990.

CHAPTER EIGHT

ONE GERMANY, ONE BERLIN

In February 1990, World War II Allies agreed to hold talks about the reunification of Germany. These negotiations, which began in March, became known as the "two-plus-four" talks because the participants were the two Germanys and the four Allied powers—the United States, France, Great Britain, and the Soviet Union. While the two-plus-four talks covered external matters that would be affected by reunification, such as Germany's borders and alliances, the two Germanys were to make decisions regarding internal affairs.

On March 18, East Germany held free parliamentary elections. A coalition of conservative parties who favored rapid unification led the vote. And on April 12, 1990, Lothar de Maizière of the Christian Democratic Party became the new premier of East Germany. Because Kohl was also a Christian Democrat, the prospects for quick and smooth unification increased.

One of De Maizière's first acts in office was to ask for forgiveness from Jews for the genocide carried out by the Nazis in World War II. While West Germany had done this years earlier, the East, under the Communists, had never acknowledged its role. Now, as West Germany had done for years, East Germany began making payments to a foundation that helped survivors of the Nazi Holocaust.

At about the same time that the death and mistreatment of millions of Jewish people was at last being recognized by the Germans, the Soviet Union announced the discovery of a mass grave believed to contain the bodies of Germans who had died in Soviet prison camps after World War II. Finally, the useless deaths of so many people were being acknowledged by those who had killed them. These confessions and admissions fueled even stronger hopes that government leaders were now ready to put Germany back together again.

Economic Union ▪ If East and West Germany were to be united, their monetary and economic systems would have to blended into one. One currency would have to convert to the other. Since West Germany had the healthy economy, and East German marks were virtually worthless outside the country's borders, it was a predrawn conclusion that all East German marks would have to be exchanged for West German marks.

East Germans reportedly had about 160 to 170 million East German marks in savings accounts, which would equal about $100 billion in West German marks if converted on a one-to-one basis. Another 17 billion East German marks were in circulation. For the West to accept the almost worthless East currency on a one-to-one basis would be a heavy financial burden. Still, the terms for the unification of the money system allowed East Germans to exchange a set amount of currency at the rate of one East German mark for one West German mark. Amounts above would be swapped at the less favorable rate of two East German marks for one West German mark. When the West German mark became the legal tender of both Germanys, all protective tariffs (taxes on imports) between the two Germanys were also to be lifted. East Germany's economy would come under the same free-market rules as West Germany's, and state-run industries were to be gradually turned over to private control.

The agreement took effect on July 1. People lined up in front of banks in the early morning hours, some standing in drenching rain, to exchange their East German money. By mid-afternoon, 3 billion marks had been exchanged nationwide. However, the exchange brought mixed emotions. Some East Germans welcomed it, while others were frightened about new economic hardships they might have to endure.

For example, one effect of the currency exchange was that poor-quality East German products went begging. East German Trabant cars, ridiculed in West Germany, were offered with rebates of 3,000 marks and still could not find buyers. East Germans had only been able to look at Western goods for more than forty years. Now, with West German marks in their pockets, they were no longer going to be denied the things they wanted so desperately—and they wanted Western products.

With such widespread rejection of anything made in East Germany, the threat to employment grew stronger each day in the East. Many East German businesses experienced large cancellations of orders. Factories with worn-out equipment and outdated production methods were now doomed to close. Under the Communist system, unemployment had been almost nonexistent. Now, however, hundreds of thousands of East Germans were facing the loss of their jobs for the first time.

By August, East Germany was sinking deeper and deeper into economic chaos. Unemployment had doubled, and industrial output was forty-two percent below the previous year. Although East Germany expected thousands of jobs to develop in new businesses in the future, workers would require training and time was needed for gearing up these industries. East German leaders, trying to head off an economic collapse, called on the West German government for more financial aid.

In spite of their dire economic picture, the East Germans were envied by other Eastern Europeans. Poles, for instance, were going through similar dramatic economic changes and had to try to make it on their own. Unlike the East Germans, who had the West Germans coming to their rescue, the Poles and other Eastern Europeans had no one to help them build a new economy.

Political Union ▪ With the economic union in place, plans for the full unification of Germany moved forward quickly. On July 2, the East German government backed a West German plan for all-German elections in 1990. In mid-July, an accord was reached to guarantee the border between the new Germany and Poland. And Gorbachev and Kohl agreed on conditions that would allow a reunified Germany to join NATO. To win the agreement, Kohl promised to limit German military strength, to allow Soviet troops to remain in East German territory for a transitional period of up to four years, and to bar the deployment of NATO troops there during that period. After that, NATO units could be assigned to the East, but nuclear weapons would not be permitted there.

With the last barrier removed, unification rushed forward. On August 23, the East German parliament formally voted to join West Germany, setting October 3 as the date. Then, on September 12, after seven months of the two-plus-four negotiations, the wartime Allies and the two Germanys signed a treaty. Under it, the Allies gave up all occupation rights and granted full sovereignty to a unified Germany. The treaty also incorporated the agreement on Soviet troop withdrawals.

Germany Unites ▪ At midnight on October 3, 1990, as the black, red, and gold flag of the Federal Republic of Germany was unfurled in front of the Reichstag building in Berlin, East Germany formally became part of West Germany. A jubilant crowd of more than one million people rejoiced in a celebration complete with the pealing of bells and the singing of national hymns. Under a hazy October moon, fireworks illuminated the Brandenburg Gate. Crowds jammed the Alexanderplatz, the broad square in the eastern half of now-unified Berlin, and splits of champagne and cans of beer were shared among the revelers.

Germany was now a single nation, with 78 million people and 137,900 square miles. Families that had been divided were now reunited, free to visit whenever they chose. Watching the celebration in Berlin, one East German woman said, "We've waited many, many years for this, to be able to live without constraints, without regulations and force. Maybe things won't be rosy at first, but the future will be better."[1] A West German man added, "It's a positive thing. It overcomes a decision that never represented the will of the people."[2] Chancellor Kohl, in a televised speech, thanked the Western Allies and especially the United States for their years of support.

Fireworks light the sky over the Brandenburg Gate in the early hours of October 3, 1990, to mark the formal reunification of Germany.

However, not all Germans were as pleased. During the celebrations in Berlin, about 5,000 demonstrators marched through the Brandenburg Gate with anti-unity banners. Some of the demonstrators broke windows, burned cars, and clashed with riot police in Alexanderplatz. Anti-unity demonstrations were held in half a dozen other German cities as well. And in many areas, the historic moment was greeted quietly. In the East, especially, concern about the hundreds of thousands of people who had lost their jobs and the uncertainty of what lay ahead kept some from participating in celebrations.

But, whether Germans chose to celebrate, protest, or simply accept it, reunification was now a fact.

Moving Ahead ▪ The German reunification agreement was nearly 1,000 pages long. But there were many details left to be decided by a new all-German parliament that would be elected in December. On December 2, 1990, Germans went to the polls in the first free all-German elections since 1932. Forty parties and groups fielded candidates, but German voters gave the Christian Democrats a resounding victory. Helmut Kohl was confirmed as the first chancellor of reunited Germany.

On December 20, the newly elected parliament met for the first time in the old Reichstag building in Berlin. Among the legislators was Willy Brandt, now aged seventy-seven. Although Berlin was now once again the formal capital of Germany, the legislature was to decide whether the government would relocate there or remain in Bonn. Brandt cast his vote for Berlin, reminding the others how the city had stood as an island of freedom within Communist East Germany. But in the end, the question was put off; and the legislature reconvened the next month in Bonn.

The question of where to locate the government was only one of many that Germany faced. Other problems, many of them inherent in bringing together people who had backgrounds in different ideologies, still remained.

One thorny issue was the files of the now-disbanded East German secret police, the Stasi. The Stasi files contained personal information about some four million East Germans and several million West Germans. The unification agreement gave the parliament the responsibility to decide the disposition of these files. Many Germans feared that the information contained in the Stasi files would fall into the wrong hands. On the other hand, former East German officials worried that they might be held to account for some of their government's actions. In a move to alleviate some of the fear of arrest for prior political activities, West Germany gave partial amnesty to former East German spies against whom judicial proceedings had not been opened and to those who would be liable for a prison sentence of less than three years.

Another problem involved real estate. Before unification, in June 1990, East Germany had agreed that property seized since 1950 would be returned or former owners would receive compensation for their losses. Early in 1991, the new German government agreed to also restore property that had been taken by the Nazis before and during World War II. But identifying and locating the former owners promised to be difficult.

Reunification also came with a heavy price tag. East Germany's roads, railroads, universities, and telephone system had to be modernized. Unemployment and other social benefits would have to paid to an estimated 1.4 million East Germans, and the withdrawal of Soviet troops from East Germany would cost billions in payments and aid. There were the costs of the currency exchange and the privatization of East German industries. In addition, the new government absorbed the debts of East Germany. In all, the costs were expected to be as high as $200 billion.

Thus the euphoria that had been so evident among the German people a year earlier was replaced with a subdued mood. Germans had begun to feel the pinch of reunification, and many of them, particularly those from the West, began to complain about the drain on their finances. East Germans, facing massive unemployment and almost complete disruption of their former lives, worried that they would be second-class citizens in the country they had fought to join. Adding to their concern was the fact that the former West German states, with a larger population, held more votes in parliament.

Meanwhile, Germany sought to allay any concerns that other nations might have about its future in Europe—concerns that, once united, Germany might try once again to dominate the continent. To a large part, those fears had subsided when it became clear that the new German government would be a reliable democracy supported by a vigorous economy.

On November 10, Mikhail Gorbachev and Chancellor Kohl signed a twenty-year nonaggression treaty in which both nations pledged to honor the borders of all European nations. Kohl remarked, ''We are closing the books on the painful past and clearing the way for a new beginning.''[3] Four days later, Germany and Poland signed a separate treaty, pledging to respect one another's borders. Germany thus made it clear that it had no ambition to regain territory it had lost as a result of defeat in World War II.

"The Cold War Is Over" ▪ In November 1990, the leaders of the Conference on Security and Cooperation in Europe (CSCE) met in Paris. The CSCE included all the nations of Europe except Albania (which had observer status), plus the United States and Canada. (This group had met in Helsinki, Finland, in 1975, and had produced the Helsinki Accords.) When French President François Mitterrand opened the 1990 summit, he said, "This is the first time in history that we witness a profound transformation of the European landscape which is not the result of war or a bloody revolution."[4]

While the future of European security and Eastern Europe's economy were the main topics of the summit, the leaders signed a document called the Charter of Paris for a New Europe. The document proclaimed an end to "the era of confrontation and division in Europe" and vowed "a new era of democracy, peace, and unity." President Bush said, "The Cold War is over. In the signing of the Charter of Paris, we have closed a chapter of history."[5]

It seemed clear that 1990 would go down in history as the year the Cold War ended. The two Germanys were reunited, and many Eastern European countries were leaving their old governments behind and moving toward democracy. (The Warsaw Pact formally disbanded on March 31, 1991.) Even the Soviet Union seemed to be moving toward permanent change. In fact, Mikhail Gorbachev won the 1990 Nobel Peace Prize. Besides encouraging the changes in Europe, Gorbachev was recognized for reducing global tension and for leading the way toward treaties that slashed conventional and nuclear forces. He had withdrawn Soviet troops from Afghanistan, freed the Soviet press, and brought more democracy to his country.

But for the Soviets, deep troubles lay ahead. Gorbachev's reforms had touched off a wave of nationalism, and several of the republics that made up the Soviet Union were beginning to demand greater independence. And while many people hoped that Gorbachev would move forward with a bold leap toward a market economy, he announced instead a cautious transition that would limit privatization and continue to allow the government to set prices. The Soviets entered the winter of 1990 facing severe food shortages. As his popularity in his own country slipped, Gorbachev took emergency powers to deal with growing economic problems and political unrest.

Germans shipped tons of food to the Soviets, a step that prompted mixed reactions. Some Soviets welcomed the aid; others, remembering Germany's invasion half a century earlier, resented it. Still others, ashamed that Germans could provide them with the things that their own government could not, were getting more unhappy with Soviet leadership.

But if the Soviet Union's future was unclear, Germany's seemed bright. Unification was accomplished. And despite all the problems they faced, Germans could look ahead to peace and prosperity.

 **EPILOGUE**

By the end of 1990, former East German leader Erich Honecker had been arrested on charges that he had personally given shoot-to-kill orders at the Berlin Wall. Too sick to be placed in jail, the architect of the Wall was eventually taken to a hospital in the Soviet Union.

Meanwhile, the once-mighty barrier was gradually being dismantled. First Berliners and tourists hacked away at the cement, many coming away with swollen knuckles and blue thumbnails. Some merely wanted a souvenir, while others began almost immediately selling bits and pieces of the Wall of Shame. Next, the Wall began to be dismantled in earnest as large cranes lifted away huge sections. Traffic jams and heavy construction equipment dominated the scene in place of armed guards.

Sections of the Wall were carted off to be ground into sand, while others were sold. There was no shortage of takers for the pieces. People from the United

*Work crews move in to tear down the Wall. A section
was left in memory of those killed trying to escape.*

States, Japan, and other countries expressed interest in obtaining sections of the Wall for souvenirs and monuments. One twelve-foot-high, 6,000-pound concrete slab was removed to become part of a monument at Westminster College in Fulton, Missouri. The work was to be dedicated to the turnaround in East-West relations. Edwina Sandys, a granddaughter of Winston Churchill and the sculptor for the memorial, hand-picked the section, which had the word *unwahr* ("untruth") scrawled across its side.

The Wall was not the only thing for sale. The watchtowers and even the guard dogs were available for a price. It was estimated that Germany might make $1 billion from these transactions. The Germans said that they would use the profits for health services and for restoration work on monuments such as the Brandenburg Gate. They also said that no section of the Wall against which someone had been shot would be sold. Still, many Germans criticized the selling of the Wall. As the barrier disappeared bit by bit and profit-making took over, they wondered how long people would remember the human lives that it had cost.

If video cameras could have captured everything that happened around the Berlin Wall during its twenty-eight-year life, the world would have a dramatic visual image of the suffering it caused. People might also have a better understanding of the forces that created the Wall and those that finally brought it down. The Berlin Wall, made of barbed wire and reinforced concrete, was also made of ignorance.

The question remains: Can people of the world cooperate to prevent future generations from going through the pain that Berlin suffered?

 NOTES

Chapter One:

1. Sulzberger, C. L., *The American Heritage Picture History of World War II.* New York: American Heritage/Bonanza Books, 1966, page 584.

Chapter Two:

1. Fontaine, Andre, *History of the Cold War.* New York: Pantheon Books, 1968, pages 276 and 277.
2. *Facts on File,* 1948, page 104.
3. *The Electronic Encyclopedia.* (Douglas Kinnard), 1988.

Chapter Four:

1. Wyden, Peter, *The Inside Story of Divided Berlin.* New York: Simon and Schuster, 1989, page 47.
2. Keller, John V., *Germany, The Wall and Berlin.* New York: Vantage Press, 1964, page 211.
3. ———, page 210.

4. Wyden, page 164.
5. ———, page 167.
6. ———, page 24.
7. Keller, page 178.

Chapter Five:

1. Wyden, page 274.

Chapter Six:

1. Wyden, page 283.
2. Brownjohn, J. Maxwell, *Willy Brandt, People and Politics: The Years 1960–1975*. Boston: Little, Brown and Company, 1976, page 91.
3. *Facts on File*, 1988, page 473.
4. *Facts on File*, 1986, page 603.

Chapter Seven:

1. *Facts on File*, "Gorbachev Visits Finland," November 3, 1989, page 821.
2. *Maclean's*, "Free at Last!" November 20, 1989, v. 102, n. 47, page 48.
3. *Newsweek*, "The Fall of the Wall," November 20, 1989, v. CXIV, n. 21, pages 28–29.
4. *Maclean's*, page 47.
5. *Newsweek*, page 39.

Chapter Eight:

1. *The New York Times*, "Two Germanys Unite after 45 Years with Jubilation and a Vow of Peace," October 3, 1990, page A1.
2. ———, page A1.
3. *Philadelphia Inquirer*, "Gorbachev, Germany OK Non-aggression Pact," November 10, 1990, page 2.
4. *Facts on File*, "CSCE Summit in Paris Finally Ends Cold War: NATO, Warsaw Pact Sign Treaty on European Arms," November 23, 1990, page 861.
5. ———, same.

 **CHRONOLOGY**

1918	November 11: World War I armistice declared
1933	Adolf Hitler becomes chancellor of Germany
1939	September 1: World War II begins as Germany invades Poland
1941	December 7: Japan attacks the United States at Pearl Harbor
	December 11: Germany and the United States declare war
1944	September 14: Western Allies enter Germany
1945	February 4–11: Yalta Conference held
	April 10: President Franklin D. Roosevelt dies; Harry S. Truman becomes president of the United States
	April 30: Death of Hitler
	May 2: Soviets capture Berlin
	May 8: Germany formally surrenders
	July 17–August 8: Potsdam Conference held
1946	March 5: Churchill makes ''Iron Curtain'' statement
1947	March 11: Truman Doctrine established
	June 5: Marshall Plan launched

1948	June 24: Soviet blockade of Berlin begins
1949	April 4: NATO created
	May 5: Federal Republic of Germany (West Germany) created
	May 11–12: Soviets lift the blockade of Berlin
	September 15: Konrad Adenauer elected chancellor of West Germany
	October 7: German Democratic Republic (East Germany) formed
1952	Dwight D. Eisenhower elected president of the United States
1953	March 5: Soviet leader Joseph Stalin dies
	June 16–17: East Berlin worker rebellions
1955	West Germany joins NATO
	May 14: Warsaw Pact formed
1956	November 4: Soviet intervention in Hungary
1957	Willy Brandt becomes mayor of West Berlin
1958	November 10: Soviet leader Nikita Khrushchev demands Allies leave Berlin
1960	John F. Kennedy elected president of the United States
1961	June 3–4: Kennedy meets with Khrushchev in Vienna; Khrushchev issues nuclear ultimatum
	August 13: Construction begins on the Berlin Wall
	October 27: Russian and American tanks face one another at Checkpoint Charlie
1962	August 17: Peter Fechter tries to escape East Berlin; his death sparks riots
1963	June 26: Kennedy's "Ich bin ein Berliner" speech
	October 16: Ludwig Erhard becomes chancellor of West Germany
	November 22: Kennedy assassinated; Lyndon Johnson takes office as president of the United States
	December 19–20: Christmas passes are issued between East and West Berlin
1964	October 14: Khrushchev removed and replaced by Leonid Brezhnev
1966	Kurt Kiesinger elected chancellor of West Germany
1968	August 20–21: Soviet troops invade Czechoslovakia

	Richard M. Nixon elected president of the United States
1969	October 21: Willy Brandt becomes chancellor of West Germany
1971	May 3: Erich Honecker replaces Ulbricht as chief executive of East Germany
	Willy Brandt awarded Nobel Peace Prize
1974	May 16: Willy Brandt resigns; Helmut Schmidt becomes chancellor of West Germany
1975	East Germany signs Helsinki Final Accord
1979	June: Salt II Treaty signed in Vienna
1981	Solidarity movement suppressed in Poland
1982	Helmut Kohl becomes chancellor of West Germany
	Brezhnev dies and is replaced by Yuri Andropov
1984	February 9: Andropov dies and is replaced by Konstantin Chernenko
1985	March 15: Mikhail Gorbachev elected first secretary of the Communist Party in Russia, following death of Chernenko
1987	September 7–11: Honecker, in first working visit to West Germany, predicts a day when borders will no longer divide the country
1989	May 2: Hungary opens its borders
	July 7–8: Gorbachev renounces Brezhnev Doctrine, which had justified the Soviet use of force in Eastern Europe
	September: New Forum is created to oppose the East German government
	October 18: Honecker is replaced by Egon Krenz; pro-democracy demonstrations in East Germany
	November 3: Czechoslovakia opens its borders
	November 9: Berlin Wall is opened
1990	July 1: Two German currencies are melded into one, leading to economic union between East and West Germany
	September 12: Four Allied nations relinquish all occupation rights in Germany following ''two-plus-four'' talks
	October 3: The two Germanys are reunified

BIBLIOGRAPHY

Abshire, David M., et. al. *Détente, Cold War Strategies in Transition*. New York: Frederick A. Praeger, 1965.

Armstrong, Anne. *Berliners, Both Sides of the Wall*. New Brunswick, New Jersey: Rutgers University Press, 1973.

Brown, Archie, and Michael Kaser. *The Soviet Union Since the Fall of Khrushchev*. New York: The Free Press, 1975.

Brownjohn, J. Maxwell. *Willy Brandt, People and Politics: The Years 1960–1975*. Boston: Little, Brown and Company, 1976.

Cate, Curtis. *The Ides of August*. New York: M. Evans and Company, Inc., 1978.

Davey, Thomas. *A Generation Divided: German Children and the Berlin Wall*. Durham: Duke University Press, 1987.

Dukes, Paul. *The Last Great Game: USA Versus USSR, Events, Conjunctures, Structures*. New York: St. Martin's Press, 1989.

Dulles, Eleanor Lansing. *Berlin: The Wall Is Not Forever*. Chapel Hill: The University of North Carolina Press, 1967.

Editors of the Army Times. *Berlin: The City That Would Not Die*. New York: Dodd, Mead & Company, 1968.

Editors of Time-Life Books. *The New Order*. Alexandria, Virginia: Time-Life Books, 1989.

Editors of Time-Life Books. *The Reach for Empire*. Alexandria, Virginia: Time-Life Books, 1989.

Editors of Time-Life Books. *The SS*. Alexandria, Virginia: Time-Life Books, 1988.

Editors of Time-Life Books. *Storming to Power*. Alexandria, Virginia: Time-Life Books, 1989.

Emerl, Sarel. *Hitler Over Europe: The Road to World War II*. Boston: Little, Brown and Company, 1972.

Facts on File *Weekly World News Digest*. New York: Facts on File, 1962–1990.

Fontaine, Andre. *History of the Cold War From the October Revolution to the Korean War 1917–1950*. New York: Pantheon Books, 1968.

Fontaine, Andre. *History of the Cold War From the Korean War to the Present*. New York: Pantheon Books, 1969.

Fitzgibbon, Constantine. *A Concise History of Germany*. New York: The Viking Press, 1972.

Fodor, Eugene. *Fodor's Germany: East and West 1987*. New York: Fodor's Travel Guides, 1986.

Galante, Pierre. *The Berlin Wall*. Garden City, New York: Doubleday & Company, Inc., 1965.

Galbraith, John Kenneth. *American Capitalism*. Boston: Houghton Mifflin Company, 1952.

Galbraith, John Kenneth, Stanislav Menshikov. *Capitalism, Communism and Coexistence*. Boston: Houghton Mifflin Company, 1988.

Gelb, Norman. *The Berlin Wall: Kennedy, Khrushchev, and a Showdown in the Heart of Europe*. New York: Times Books, 1986.

Goldston, Robert. *The Life and Death of Nazi Germany*. New York: The Bobbs-Merrill Company, Inc., 1967.

Grunfeld, Frederic V., and the Editors of Time-Life Books. *Berlin*. Amsterdam: Time-Life Books, 1977.

Heaps, Willard A. *The Wall of Shame*. New York: Duell, Sloan, and Pearce, 1964.

Holbrook, Sabra. *Germany, East & West.* New York: Meredith Press, 1968.

James, Harold. *A German Identity.* New York: Routledge, Chapman, and Hall Inc., 1989.

Keffe, Eugene, et. al. *Area Handbook for the Federal Republic of Germany.* Washington: U.S. Government Printing Office, 1975.

Keller, John W. *Germany, The Wall and Berlin: Internal Politics During an International Crisis.* New York: Vantage Press, 1964.

Kelman, Steven. *Behind the Berlin Wall.* Boston: Houghton Mifflin Company, 1972.

Laqueur, Walter. *The Long Road to Freedom: Russia and Glasnost.* New York: Charles Scribner's Sons, 1989.

MacCloskey, Monro. *The Infamous Wall of Berlin.* New York: Richards Rosen Press, Inc., 1967.

Ninkovich, Franklin. *Germany and the United States.* Boston: Twayne Publishers, 1988.

Schick, Jack M. *The Berlin Crisis 1958–1962.* Philadelphia: University of Pennsylvania Press, 1971.

Sulzberger, C. L. *The American Heritage Picture History of World War II.* New York: American Heritage/Bonanza Books, 1966.

Turner, Jr., Henry Ashby. *The Two Germanies Since 1945.* London: Yale University Press, 1987.

Tusa, John and Ann. *The Berlin Airlift.* New York: Atheneum, 1988.

Von Nesselrode, Franz. *Germany's Other Half.* London: Abelard-Schuman, 1963.

Wyden, Peter. *Wall: The Inside Story of Divided Berlin.* New York: Simon and Schuster, 1989.

 **RECOMMENDED READING**

Collier, Richard. *Bridge Across the Sky.* McGraw Hill, 1978.

Dolan, Edward. *Victory in Europe: The Fall of Hitler's Germany.* Watts, 1988.

Dudman, John. *The Division of Berlin.* Rourke, 1988.

Galante, Pierre. *The Berlin Wall.* Doubleday, 1965.

Gelb, Norman. *The Berlin Wall: Kennedy, Khrushchev, and a Showdown in the Heart of Europe.* Times Books, 1986.

Gross, Leonard. *The Last Jews in Berlin.* Bantam Books, 1982.

Mee, Charles L. *Meeting at Potsdam.* M. Evans, 1975.

Pimlott, John. *The Cold War.* Watts, 1987.

Westerfeld, Scott. *The Berlin Airlift.* Silver Burdett, 1989.

INDEX